QUALITY
TENNIS
AFTER 50 ...
OR 60 ...
OR 70 ...
OR .....

QUALITY TENNIS AFTER 50 ...
OR 60 ...
OR 70 ...
OR .....

PETER SCHWED

INTRODUCTION BY BOBBY RIGGS

ST. MARTIN'S PRESS   NEW YORK

Design by Jaye Zimet

Library of Congress Cataloging-in-Publication Data

Schwed, Peter.
    Quality tennis after 50— or 60— or 70— or— / Peter Schwed ;
introduced by Bobby Riggs.
        p.   cm.
    ISBN 0-312-04312-0
    1. Tennis. 2. Middle aged persons—Recreation. I. Title.
II. Title: Quality tennis after 50 . . . or 60 . . . or 70 . . . or . . .
GV995.S3565   1990   89-77644
796.342′0240565—dc20   CIP

First Edition

10 9 8 7 6 5 4 3 2 1

Once again, for dear
ANTONIA
a.k.a.
TONI
my doubles partner in life

CONTENTS

PART III GETTING CAGEY: ADAPTING YOUR STROKES AND STRATEGY

INTRODUCTION

It's obvious that back in 1939 when I was the number-
one player in the world, winner of all three Wimbledon
titles (singles, doubles, mixed doubles) and the United
States championship as well, my name would be well
known—at least to tennis fans. More surprising, but
just about as gratifying, is that today, more than fifty
years later, actually more people are aware of me and
my tennis than back then. Of course, the main reason
for this was the much publicized circuses that Margaret
Smith Court and Billie Jean King and I put on in the
two "battles of the sexes," but even without those I've
been able to make my mark as a veteran tennis player
who hasn't just quietly faded away, as old soldiers are
reputed to do. Starting in the 45-and-older division,
and running in stages through each subsequent five-
year category—the 50s, 55s, 60s, 65s—I've won over
thirty national titles and am still doing so now in my
70s.

That is why this new book of Peter Schwed's has
a particular appeal for me. It's aimed at enthusiastic
tennis players who want to continue to have fun, playing the best tennis of which they're capable, right

through their entire lives. If I'd thought of it before Peter did, and had wanted to take enough time off from playing tennis to sit down and write such a book, I might have done so myself instead of just writing an introduction for this one. Oh well, I got in a lot of good tennis while Peter was pounding away at his typewriter!

In any event, this is a dandy book. It's enthusiastic, instructive, and consistently fun to read throughout. No two tennis buffs agree about everything involved in the game, so now and then I might not go along completely with an idea that Peter expresses, but that's natural. I'm every bit as opinionated as he admits to being at certain spots in his book where he confesses he holds unorthodox views about traditional tennis gospel, but I wouldn't argue that he might not be right. For here are the opinions and thoughts and advice of a true tennis player, not just somebody who happens to play tennis. There is solid and useful information here that ranges from physical conditioning and equipment suggestions, through techniques of stroking and tactics, to ways of expanding your opportunities for playing senior tennis, both in your local community and elsewhere in the country.

This is definitely no dry instruction manual. Schwed's writing style is so amiable and lighthearted, and his views so interesting and provocative, that his book can be read for sheer fun by any tennis player, even some who are younger than 50. It's a book they'll want to keep around until their day comes!

—BOBBY RIGGS

x

PART I

WHY "AFTER 50," AND WHAT IS "QUALITY TENNIS"?

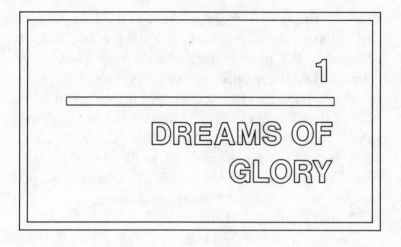

1

DREAMS OF GLORY

One of my favorite stories (which I admittedly have recounted before in at least one other book, but who's counting?) has to do with when I was a teenager, long, long ago, and it would seem from the following that I must have been a pretty dewy-eyed one. I was at home one day, reading an extremely saccharine novel that impressed my youthful romantic fancy so much that, when I hit a particularly sugary passage, I claimed the attention of my considerably older brother and his friend, who also happened to be reading in the same room. I asked if I could read a short but very moving excerpt to them, one I thought well worth the discourtesy of disturbing them at their own reading. Both looked at me a little owlishly but they politely agreed, and I started to read from my own book in a hushed and reverent voice.

It would take a good deal of inane research today

to try to dig up a copy of A. A. Milne's *Two People*, and I have no intention of undertaking the task. I remember the passage in the book well enough to suffice. Mr. Milne, the whimsical creator of Winnie the Pooh, had one of the characters in this novel pontificate that if a person could dictate the ideal life, it would be to be a famous athlete from the age of 15 to 25; a beautiful woman from 25 to 35; a dashing explorer-adventurer from 35 to 45; a world-famous author from 45 to 55; a distinguished statesman from 55 to 65; and a gardener from 65 to 75.

I'm sure I haven't got it exactly right after all these years, but that's close enough. The punch line about the gardener is completely accurate. Anyhow, there was a moment of silence after I read the passage, and I looked up for a reaction. I got it. My brother's friend commented ever so mildly, "It seems to me that there'd be more kick in it to be a famous *athlete* from 65 to 75!"

It was a very funny riposte, but I never thought about it as anything other than a gag until I reached some age around 50. That's when I started to receive tennis publications that listed tournaments all over the place for various age groups: singles, doubles, mixed doubles, father and son and mother and daughter tournaments, father and daughter and mother and son tournaments, community team matches, league affairs. I had always been a good, but not brilliant school, college, and club tennis player, and had even won a couple of silver-plated cups along the way, which were now gathering dust in a closet, but those triumphs had been a long time ago. But look here! Maybe I could be a famous athlete in a recognized tournament where the competitors were all my own ripe age? Maybe?

I'll give away the answer right now at the beginning. I never did become a famous athlete at 65, but I did learn a lot and had a lot of fun playing senior tennis, and it led me to write a book that I hope will be both helpful and entertaining for others—this book.

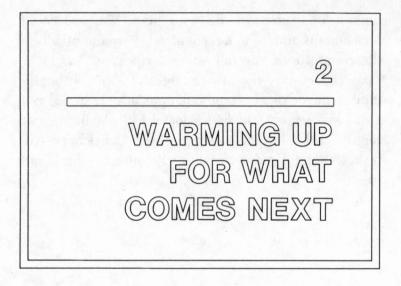

2

WARMING UP FOR WHAT COMES NEXT

You might ask why the first, and thus apparently the important, age in the title is 50. That's a good question because much of what this book will cover is more specifically directed at a player who is in his or her 60s, or even considerably older than that. (I'm going to use the "him or her" locution as infrequently as possible from now on, since it can drive both an author and a reader crazy. From now on, please accept the fact that "his" is used in the inclusive sense, and means "his or her" every time. Tennis is not a respecter of persons or of sex.)

Where were we? Oh, yes. Sometime in one's 60s is when most experienced tennis players really feel that they're not quite what they used to be, whereas a healthy player still in his 50s is often not likely to feel that way at all. He may still prefer to play singles, continuing to beat the people he always has been able to beat in the past, even though many of them are years, and even decades, younger. This book isn't going to be particularly meaningful to such a player, although it may interest or amuse him.

So why *did* I choose 50 as the age at which readers might be attracted to the book, and benefit from it? Well, although lots of over-50 players are as good as they ever were, even more recognize that they are not, though they may be reluctant to admit it. Sooner or later—and it may well be in one's 50s—to every tennis player there comes a moment when, if he is wise, he will reevaluate his game and his attitude toward it. Even if you don't feel you have slipped at all, or not enough to matter much, it is wise to prepare yourself for the inevitable time when you'll be playing tennis somewhat differently.

But don't let that discourage you. You can play tennis just as enthusiastically and very probably more enjoyably than in the past, and if you've lost something in physical ability, you may well compensate for it by being that much wiser and cagier. The time to learn the tricks of continuing to be a quality tennis player, in your 60s and later, is when you're in your 50s and see it coming. The financial adviser to a person who is going to retire doesn't wait until his client cleans out his desk for the last time and starts for home. Plans and investments are all worked over and the ground-work activated long before the big day when the retiree receives his gold watch and a handshake. When a baseball manager senses that he's going to have to call on a relief pitcher, he doesn't wait until the situation becomes so critical that the relief picher has to take the mound and start flinging fast balls toward a menacing batter right away. No—the manager has him warm up in the bullpen for quite a while first.

In like manner, a tennis player in his mid-50s will be ahead of the Fates if he learns then to adopt fresh attitudes to the game and himself. He should be maintaining the best physical condition of which he's capable or, at least, acceptably good physical well-being. He should study and put into practice the more subtle techniques of stroking and tactics. That way, when he is 65, let's say, and not at all ready to retire to the rocking chair, he'll still be playing well enough to be welcome in any game of his peers. Nor does he necessarily need to be limited to that. A solid, capable, smart old player is often a much more desirable doubles partner than a slam-bang, flashy young one, and can be welcome in quite high-caliber doubles matches. (I am referring to doubles because that's the game to which we all gravitate at some point, and properly so.)

I know that what I write above is true because eight of us have had a weekend doubles event going for many years, consisting of two matches going on side by side on adjacent courts. In our two hours of reserved time, we invariably get in three sets, changing partners and opponents to get the best mix possible. We prearrange this so as not to waste time between sets discussing each new setup. Well, the point is that among our basic eight players, and some fifty players we know who are eager to pinch-hit whenever any of us can't play, we have players ranging from 18 to 80! And there's no one who can't hold up his end in a friendly but very competitive match. Those two hours represent a high spot of the week both for our high school players and for our grandfather players, which says a lot about the love of tennis.

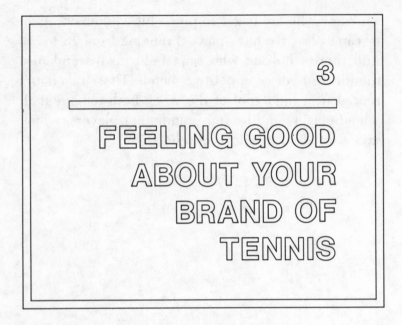

3
FEELING GOOD ABOUT YOUR BRAND OF TENNIS

The joy of falling in love with tennis is, for those who encounter it, second only to the more traditional experience of love, celebrated by poets and the film industry. (There are some rabidly fanatical people who might not rank tennis love as low as second place but, tennis aficionado that I be, I am not of their number.) But a similar and very happy aspect of love for tennis is that one can be bitten by the bug at just about any age. Although there are tremendously ambitious parents, dreaming of future glory on the courts for their progeny, who thrust cut-down racquets into the hands of 4- or 5-year-olds and send them off to tennis camp, I don't approve even if there are claims that it sometimes works. It's wiser and better, I believe, to abstain from offering this great gift of potential years of joy until your child is of an age really to appreciate it and grab on to it for a lifetime. I'd say that would be at about 7 or 8, but maybe that's because it was then that I myself was introduced to the great game. I suspect that a child can't truly be much interested in, let alone fall in love with, any sport that calls for competitiveness and the keeping of a score until he or she is able to run and jump and throw a ball with at least modest competence. That's in addition to having enough familiarity with numbers to be at all intrigued with keeping score. Seven or 8 would be about it.

On the other side of the coin, any age is fine for older players. Of course most tennis players take up the game and develop and flourish through school and college and during the years right afterward, but despite their having loved the game, too many of them quit playing when they reach 40 or 45. Except for someone who has suffered some major physical injury or illness that has ruled out future play, I've never met any tennis dropouts in later years who didn't regret doing so, but now felt it was too late to take up the game again.

They were wrong. Just as it's possible to fall in love more than once, you can take up tennis again after years of inaction on the court and find yourself not only enjoying it but doing well to boot. Surely it's easier to do this than to start playing tennis for the first time at a rather mature age. Yet today there are multitudes of men and women packing both public

11

and private courts who, inspired by the tennis boom of the past twenty years, played the game for the first time when they were 40 or well past that age. Many became very admirable players in a remarkably short time, but even those who didn't, belong with what is perhaps the most devoted crowd of all, as far as playing tennis after 50 is concerned. They've truly fallen in love, and like the old song, they've fallen in love with love as well. They may have taken up tennis for some dull reason, like losing a little weight, or thinking a tennis outfit was fetching, or because everybody important was doing it, but they soon found themselves seduced by the ecstatic pleasure of hitting a winning cross-court drive. In other words, some are born to tennis, some achieve it, and some have it thrust upon them.

Two conclusions, then, can be drawn from the preceding discussion. The first is that one cannot tell what sort of person may become so enamored of the game as to be ardently desirous of continuing to play it at every opportunity, not only after 50 but at any age at all, no matter how elderly. The famous case that's often cited is Gustav V of Sweden, who played constantly right up until the time of his death at age 92, but there is better and perhaps even more impressive evidence closer at hand. C. Alphonso Smith, who has won national titles in every age group in which he has competed since he was a schoolboy, is now just 81 and is still winning them—and handily. He's still so devastating a player that he'll beat almost any player a quarter of a century younger than he who might innocently wander out onto the courts at Charlottesville, Virginia, where he holds sway. President of Super-Senior Tennis, Inc., an organization devoted to the promotion of tennis for seniors aged 55–85 (and I'd wager they'll increase that upper limit when Smith passes it!), he puts out a bimonthly newsletter that is circulated to almost three thousand members, who pay dues of twelve dollars a year. Smith was honored a few years ago as being the only person ever to win national titles fifty years apart.

Then there is the astonishing Dorothy ("Dodo") Bundy Cheney, who was recognized as one of the world's best women players back in the 1930s and '40s when she was young, and has gained even more fame in the years after she passed 40. Since then she has won virtually every tournament she has entered and now, at the age of 73, has amassed close to two hundred national championship titles, far more than any other tennis player in history has ever achieved. Dodo Cheney today is a lead-pipe cinch to win any event for her age group. She makes things a little more interesting by dropping down and entering tournaments for the next age group younger than she, or the one even younger than that, and she wins in those classes too!

Gardnar Mulloy is another outstanding Golden Oldie, with almost one hundred U.S. Tennis Association gold balls to his credit. A great enough singles player back in the 1940s and '50s to have reached the finals one year in the U.S. championships at Forest Hills, Mulloy was even better known as a doubles specialist. He and Billy Talbert formed a virtually unbeatable

C. ALPHONSO SMITH

14

DOROTHY ("DODO") CHENEY (STEPHEN SZURLEJ/*TENNIS* MAGAZINE)

15

GARDNAR MULLOY

16

doubles combination during that era. Mulloy is almost 77 years old now, and is generally acknowledged to be the best player of that age ever to wield a racquet. He has been ranked number one for years in several senior age divisions.

Sarah Palfrey Danzig belongs in here too. Starting in 1926 she won national titles over a forty-three-year period, including the U.S. singles in 1941 and 1945, and she won the national women's doubles nine times in a twelve-year span, with four different partners. Her last title came in the senior mixed doubles hard-court championship at Seattle in 1969, when she was part-nered with C. Alphonso Smith. If severe arthritis hadn't hit her after that, eventually requiring a hip replace-ment, she would still be knocking over most of the competition today, at the age of 77. For she played in a fairly high-level *World Tennis* weekly doubles game for twenty years, only stopping two years ago when she had to undergo a second hip replacement. But when you're truly in love with the game of tennis, as Sarah has always been, you're in love for keeps, so she religiously umpires that weekly doubles game every Tuesday!

The second conclusion that can be drawn from the preceding is that my definition of "quality tennis," or a quality player, is intended to be very loose as far as this book is concerned. You're probably familiar with the National Tennis Rating Program (NTRP), but in case you are not, here it is:

1.0 This player is just starting to play tennis.
1.5 This player has limited experience and is

still working primarily on getting the ball into play.

2.0 This player needs on-court experience. This player has obvious stroke weaknesses but is familiar with basic positions for singles and doubles play.

2.5 This player is learning to judge where the ball is going, although court coverage is weak. This player can sustain a rally of slow pace with other players of the same ability.

3.0 This player is consistent when hitting medium-paced shots, but is not comfortable with all strokes and lacks control when trying for directional intent, depth, or power.

3.5 This player has achieved improved stroke dependability and direction on moderate shots, but still lacks depth and variety. This player is starting to exhibit more aggressive net play, has improved court coverage, and is developing teamwork in doubles.

4.0 This player has dependable strokes, including directional intent and depth on both forehand and backhand sides on moderate shots, plus the ability to use lobs, overheads, approach shots, and volleys with some success. This player occasionally forces errors when serving and teamwork in doubles is evident.

4.5 This player has begun to master the use of power and spins and is beginning to handle pace, has sound footwork, can control depth of shots, and is beginning to vary tactics according to opponents. This player can hit first serves with power and accuracy and place the second serve, and is able to rush the net successfully.

5.0 This player has good shot anticipation and frequently has an outstanding shot or exceptional consistency around which a game may be structured. This player can regularly hit winners or force errors off of short balls and can put away volleys; can successfully execute lobs, drop shots, half volleys, and overhead smashes; and has good depth and spin on most second serves.

5.5 This player has developed power and/or consistency as a major weapon. This player can vary strategies and styles of play in a competitive situation and hits dependable shots in a stress situation.

6.0 This player will generally not need a NTRP rating. Rankings or past rankings will speak for themselves. The 6.0 player typically has had intensive training for national tournament competition at the junior level and collegiate levels and has obtained a sectional and/or national ranking.

6.5 This player has a reasonable chance of succeeding at the **7.0** level and has extensive satellite tournament experience.

7.0 This is a world-class player who is committed to tournament competition on the international level and whose major source of income is tournament prize winnings.

Studying the NTRP rating categories, one could very logically come to the conclusion that anybody with a rating of less than 4.5 or 5.0 could not conceivably be thought of as a genuine quality player, and that true quality exists only at the 6.5 and 7.0 levels. That is indeed one way of looking at matters, but it's the wrong way with respect to your being able to play quality tennis after 50, and this is why.

No one is expecting you to be a contender for the Wimbledon or U.S. Open championships if you are over 50. All that is expected of you, and all that you should realistically wish for yourself, is to continue to play tennis and, very particularly, to enjoy it by reason of playing extremely well by *your* standards. Let's say you're a 4.0 player. That would mean you've achieved a very respectable level of casual weekend play and, in local town tournaments, can probably win a round or two, if you get a favorable draw, before losing very convincingly to one of the town's stars, a 5.0 player.

But maybe *not* so convincingly. As sometimes happens when you play an opponent considerably better than yourself, your game may be inspired and you may play over your head, so to speak. It's very doubtful that you can play well enough to win, but you may play at about a 4.5 level, actually making things close enough to give your superior opponent some nasty moments. When that happens—and it can happen quite frequently once you accept the idea that the next higher level is not beyond your grasp and you can achieve it sometimes, if not consistently—you are playing *your* standard of quality tennis. Whereas the 5.0 player, who normally would not allow you more than a couple of games in two sets, but who becomes tentative and cautious as you win two games by midway in the first set, may go on to win anyway, 6-3, 6-3, but *he* has not played quality tennis even though it's still considerably better than yours.

So quality tennis is what makes *you* feel good about yourself, and if you can manage to play it, at whatever level, you'll be enjoying yourself. An astute poet-philosopher once wrote something very apropos about legitimate pride and satisfaction in one's performance within one's own sphere:

> Life liveth best in life,
> And chooseth not to roam
> If all be well at home.
> *"Solid as ocean foam!"*
> Quoth ocean foam.

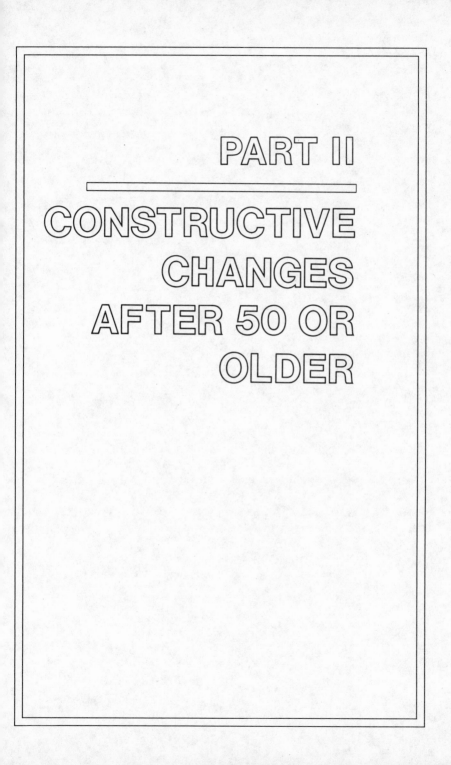

PART II

CONSTRUCTIVE CHANGES AFTER 50 OR OLDER

A BRIEF DIGRESSION

Before we venture into specifics, it might be wise to pause a moment and think about whether you actually *want* to play serious tennis in the years after you've reached 50 . . . or 60 . . . or 70 . . . or whatever. Let's face it. A lot of estimable citizens who once played tennis, and perhaps played it well and eagerly in their athletic prime, laid down their racquets permanently at quite an early age. They did so either to retire to what they think are greener pastures, known as golf courses, or to some lesser form of recreation, or they just retired. Is it possible you have a languorous inclination to be of their number?

That's fair enough if you have a medical reason (other than torpor), but if not I can cite one powerful reason why you shouldn't. Continuing to play the best tennis of which you're capable throughout the latter years of your life invariably turns out to be the closest thing to the Fountain of Youth that man or woman has yet discovered.

In any event, consider what your other options are. You certainly don't want to vegetate after 50, or 60, or whatever age happens to mark a falling-off point physically for you. You don't want to decline either in mind or in body if you can help it. Continuing to keep alert and busy and curious about the world around you is the best medicine for staving off mental vegetation, but what's the best activity for keeping you on your toes physically as well as mentally? Tennis gets my vote—so long as it's quality tennis of the best brand you can deliver, played with heart and wisdom and enthusiasm.

What about the other popular individual participant sport—golf? Undeniably golf is a wonderful game too, and undeniably it's easier on an aging body, but isn't it perhaps somewhat *too* easy? Walking is really the only exercise you get out of a round of golf, and in these plush days you're likely to be seduced into using a golf cart whether you want one or not, because everyone else is using one. When that happens you can't say you're getting any real exercise at all. Swinging a golf club about 70 times if you're a scratch golfer (and half of them being putts), or about 140 times if you're a duffer, is apt to be less exercise than shopping for the groceries. Also, unless you can afford to travel to where the sun shines all year, and wish to do so, golf is at best a six-month game for those who live in northern climates. That used to be true of tennis too, but no longer. Indoor tennis courts abound all over the nation, and January is just as good a month for your regular weekend game as July.

Swimming, performed seriously, is perhaps the best of all sports for a person physically, but its joys also depend largely on climate. (For swimming in indoor pools, unless you're a *real* swimmer willing and able to maintain form and speed and flip turns lap after lap after lap, is for most of us boring, boring, boring.) If you just get into the water and swim awhile, and then turn over on your back and float awhile, and then climb out and towel off and lie down awhile, which is the way almost all of us "swim," you may be passing the time pleasantly enough, and getting a tan, but not much more. Also, there's a fundamental drawback to this sort of swimming that applies to a number of other physical activities that admittedly can be good exercise, such as stationary bicycles, rowing machines, Nautilus machines, and the like. They do offer a person effective ways to achieve and maintain condition, but closets and attics and garages all over the country abound with deserted equipment and gear of this type, and the basic reason is that interest in a sporting activity generally flags quickly if it doesn't involve competition and keeping a score. You don't always have to win to become deeply involved with a sport, but you do need some spur, like competition, to keep going over a long period of time. Exercise machines and (alas!) casual swimming and jogging don't provide that, while tennis and golf do. However, we've already faulted golf as the best sports pursuit for seniors, so that leaves tennis as the outstanding candidate for your involvement and your affection. To bring this digression to a close, let's now hope that you *do want* to play tennis regularly now and in the years to come, and let's move on to the serious business of how you can best play quality tennis.

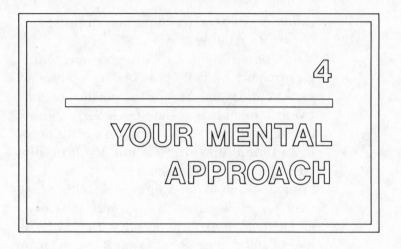

4

YOUR MENTAL APPROACH

The peculiar (and nice) thing about deciding just how you should gear your sights in order to play your most enjoyable tennis after 50 is that you have options all the way. The correct choice for you may be the exact opposite of the equally sensible choice made by your longtime tennis companion, even though you're the same age and have always played neck-and-neck matches against each other. There are five important areas of choice that the older tennis player would do well to ponder over, and each one offers considerable variety:

1. Your mental approach to enabling yourself to play the best game of which you are capable at this stage of your life. That is the subject of this chapter.
2. Your physical approach to keeping in reasonable shape despite any existing deterio-

ration of your body's condition, or prospects of further trouble ahead.

3. Your contentment with your present tennis equipment, or your possible inclination to explore the wonders—or the perils—of late-twentieth-century state-of-the-art tennis racquets, gear, shoes, warm-up suits, et cetera ad infinitum. Areas 2 and 3 will be discussed in the next chapter.

4. Your decision about going along with whatever you now possess in the way of strokes and tactics, or experimenting with new techniques and strategies, and your decision about whether to concentrate from now on almost exclusively on doubles, the thinking person's game. These topics are discussed in chapters 7 and 8.

5. Your satisfaction in continuing to play with your regular tennis opponents and partners, or your appetite for venturing into new fields of competition and new opportunities for companionship. These subjects are discussed in the final chapter.

Let's look into each of these five areas one by one, evaluating the various options they offer. In each case bear in mind that the choices you make are not necessarily the ones that would win a consensus vote from others in your position. No—each person is best suited to chart his own course. As Rudyard Kipling once put it:

There are nine and sixty ways
Of constructing tribal lays,
And every single one of them is right!

It won't do to sit still, however, for things do start to get different—sometimes extremely different—for a player once he reaches a particular age. That age may be 50 or considerably later, and it can frequently be earlier. Anyhow, when it arrives, it's time to start constructing your own specific tribal lay, so now let's review the factors in each option that enable us to make a choice.

What about your mental approach? Have you any realistic expectations that your tennis proficiency after 50 will continue to be of the same caliber as it was before? A ranked player will surely have lost his fine edge at 50, but an accomplished local tournament or club player is quite likely to be just about as good as ever at that age. But at some time everybody inevitably slows up. The great players feel the change before they're 35, but ordinary players like you and me are more likely not to feel, or at least not to acknowledge, any significant change in our accustomed game until along about 60. However, the great player (like Jimmy Connors) continues to play quality tennis by his lights, and so can the ordinary player (you and I) by our own respective standards. What one needs is a new mental approach to the game, and selecting a constructive one can open vistas that may enrich your enjoyment of tennis past anything you've experienced in your previous life on the courts.

The first sign of change in the older player's attitude toward the game is his sneaky feeling that competitive singles isn't quite the fun it used to be—that it has become something unpleasantly similar to hard work. This is particularly true if he is starting to be

31

hard pressed by, and even losing to, players he's been accustomed to beating handily in the past. Simultaneously he discovers that doubles, a form of tennis that heretofore he has always considered something of a garden-party pastime, is actually a lot of fun. Doubles allows you to make enough of the same ego-inflating good shots you're accustomed to feel are your due; allows you to preen yourself as a winner when your team wins, but softens the pain of losing when your team loses (because no one can really pin the blame for a loss specifically on one player or the other); makes for good companionship; and leaves you nothing like so short of breath as does singles.

It is admittedly something of a wrench for a person who has dearly loved the singles game, and has been cool toward, if not actually scornful of, the less demanding physical character of the doubles game, to change his sights. He may not be ready to do so at 50, but he will . . . he will. And here's the good news. Once a tennis enthusiast really gets into doubles and the multiple cooperative tactics, ploys, and stratagems that an imaginative pair of partners can employ, doubles is more pure *fun* than singles. So deciding to concentrate on doubles may well be the first option you choose in reviewing possible changes in your mental attitudes toward tennis.

The second change is one that you should resist, and when you do, something beneficial can emerge. Let's say that you're still playing competitive singles. Even well before you really feel it's time to stop, there may come a stage in your tennis career when you allow your competitive spark to flicker, and you start settling for the satisfaction of having played pretty well, of having made a respectable showing. That's an understandable enough reaction in one way. Perhaps realistically you had no chance of beating a younger and better opponent, and you did well to make a contest of it. But mentally you should never abandon the idea of winning, for it's possible that if you play things smart, and have a little luck thrown in as well, you can sometimes pull off an upset.

A mid-course tactic is the one to adopt. If your opponent hits certain shots that you once could handle well but now can barely reach—if at all—the answer is to let him win them outright, *but concentrate even harder than usual on winning the next point*! After all, the chances are that he won't be able to hit that sort of sure-winner shot more frequently than once every game or two—most regular club-level players can't. Okay. Concede those points when they come zooming past you, and applaud your opponent with a tap of your racquet or a call of "Nice shot!" But don't wear yourself out, and break your heart futilely, in attempts to run down every shot that you never could turn into a winner once in fifty attempts. Now you need to conserve your energy. Save it for the point you do have a chance to win—which is the very next point. In a way, you are living to fight another day, or at least another point. After all, losing a point every game, or possibly every other game, is by no means an insurmountable handicap. You can very possibly overcome it with your own good or lucky shot, or your opponent's poor or unlucky shot. But even if you can't, you've continued to hang in there fighting: you haven't been content merely to make a fairly respectable showing. Conceding a point now and then when the point is almost irrevocably lost anyhow, but trying your utmost all the rest of the way, is quality tennis, whether you win or lose in the end. Conceding defeat mentally, but being smug about playing rather well, is not true quality tennis, and it's never really very satisfying and enjoyable either.

Another aspect of one's mental approach to playing tennis in later years belongs more in the strategy section than it does here, so at this point I'll just hint at it. Is it wise to continue to try to play the most consistent, error-free tennis of which you're capable (if that's the sort of player you've always been), or continue to play a hard-hitting, net-rushing, gambling sort of game (if that has been your forte up to now)? Or might it be wiser, if revolutionary, to throw past methods to the winds and adopt completely different techniques and strategies? It's possible the latter course would be wise and at least equally possible that it wouldn't, but you ought to think about it. Regardless of what type of player you've been, as a senior player your circumstances both of mind and body may well have altered enough that you now have a choice to make that could be fundamental with respect to your playing and enjoying quality tennis in the future. As indicated, there will be more about this a little later on.

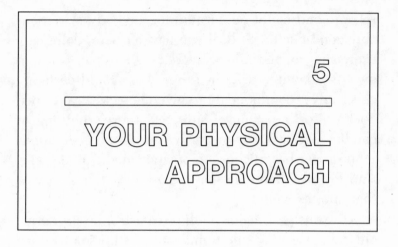

5

YOUR PHYSICAL APPROACH

How you feel physically may have a lot to do with how realistic your tennis ambitions are once you're past 50, so let's put you on the scale and look you over. But let me emphasize that this chapter is no more than one nonmedical man's suggestions, based on his own personal experiences in over half a century of regular tennis playing. I've coped with sprains, strains, pulled ligaments, breaks, aching knees, elbows, and feet, and just about all the calamities, mostly minor but some major, that plague tennis players, including being overweight at times. I've done a lot of reading in the sports medicine field and I'll try to put in capsule form some of it that has impressed me, but most of the advice here stems from the empirical—relying on my own observation and experiments, and discovering what works best for me. It might work well for you too, and I've been reassured by doctor friends that nothing I recommend could be harmful for anybody in reasonably good health. Still, if you haven't been doing any exercising, or haven't been treating any pain with an over-the-counter drug or salve, you should certainly check any recommendations given here with your own doctor. You must make sure that there's nothing in conflict with your own particular physical situation. Your doctor has a license to practice medicine; I don't. And for all I know he may be a better tennis player than me, as well!

Obviously, a major medical catastrophe or a crippling disease may rule tennis out of a person's future life, but not necessarily even then. Billy Talbert had to take insulin shots for his diabetes during matches right through his brilliant career. There are lots of tennis players, many of advanced age, who continue playing serious and good tennis once they have recovered from a heart attack—even after bypass surgery. I know a couple who play with as much intensity as they ever did, with heart pacemakers ticking away steadily inside. People with vision almost obscured by cataracts have an implant operation and within a few weeks see all life, and particularly tennis balls, better than ever before. There are persons devoted to tennis who have had an artificial hip replacement, and who get back onto the court and play acceptably, even if they can't cover down-the-line shots the way they once did. There's no end to such stories about courage and determination, but generally most of us are more likely to be troubled by some form of arthritis, moderate or severe, than anything else.

Arthritis is a disease that, in some form, affects

almost everybody, in varying degrees, as they age. It certainly wasn't affecting Vic Seixas when he won the Wimbledon singles championship in 1953 and the United States title the following year. Seixas continued to play world-class tennis for some years after that, but when he hit his 60s, the pain in both knees, which had been building up for some time, became so intense that he was afraid he'd have to give up completely the game he loved so much. Even walking had become difficult, but Seixas followed the advice of the well-known orthopedist Dr. Charles B. Goodwin, and didn't go into a shell or act like an invalid. Instead he developed an exercise program, kept his knees warm with elastic bandages and wraps while playing, stayed within the limits he could tolerate, and experimented with what he could achieve in his play. Little by little, that program enabled Seixas to return to competitive tennis of championship caliber, and in 1988 he teamed with Bobby Riggs to win the USTA national indoor doubles championship in the 65-and-older class.

Exercise programs such as Seixas undertook don't have to be strenuous or energetic, or even time-consuming, to work miracles with a physique that has been allowed to deteriorate for years and has picked up some arthritis to boot. I'd like to tell you about one that particularly impressed me.

Back in 1975, when I was a book publisher, I was the editor of a book that became the nation's number-one nonfiction bestseller for many months. Its title was *Total Fitness in 30 Minutes a Week*, and while at first glance that title may give a false impression—that you can become totally fit very quickly—it isn't deceitful because the authors' thesis is that even if you haven't exercised once in the last twenty years, you are only two hours away from good physical condition. What they meant by the figure in the title was that after only four weeks of spending merely thirty minutes a week on their program, you'd be in good shape. You'd actually feel better after just one week, and if you continued the program after four weeks and stepped it up, you would enjoy even greater benefits. But for a mere four weeks, spending ten minutes a day three times a week produces a wonderful effect. The book was a collaborative effort, with Dr. Laurence E. Morehouse of UCLA, an outstanding authority on physical education and sports medicine, supplying the material, which Leonard Gross then whipped into a professional manuscript.

I was so impressed with the book that I started the exercise program myself, and whenever I feel that I've let myself get flabby or stiff (which over the years has happened more often than I care to confess), I go back to the program and, for four weeks, put myself through the very easy paces outlined as the starting point. The fact is that I never did try to go past those early stages and attempt to become Mr. Universe, because those rather gentle, easy, and nonburdensome actions were enough to make me feel alert and flexible again after a month or so. If you are more ambitious than I am, I'd suggest you get hold of that admirable book, which, almost fifteen years after it was originally published, is still in print and going strong in a paperback edition published by Pocket Books.

In the meantime, here's a brief digest of Morehouse's instructions concerning the initial steps to fitness, which is as far as I intend to take you, since our goal is a modest one. We are not in training for the next Olympics, but we would like to take whatever wreck of a physique we may now have and make it a lot better. This simple regimen will do the trick.

Divide each ten-minute exercise session into three parts:

1. *One minute of limbering (see page 40)*. First, on your toes, stretch as high as you can toward the ceiling, first with one arm and then the other. Second, with arms extended to the side, twist your trunk as far as it will go, first in one direction and then in the other. Third, lean over, grasp each leg behind the knee, and pull your shoulders down gently toward your knees. Don't jerk or use force—just stretch in an easy pull. If you can get your shoulders even close to your knees you're already pretty supple; if you can't get even close, don't worry about it. Do this a few more times in the days to come and you will get closer and meanwhile you're doing yourself a lot of good. Finally, stretch your neck muscles by gently turning your head a little bit farther than it can turn on its own. Turn it to the left by putting your left hand underneath the right-hand side of your chin, and your right hand over your left ear. Push your left hand gently to the left and your right hand gently to the right; this will enable you to turn your head—*gently*, please!—the distance you wish to achieve. Then reverse the process and turn your head a bit farther to the right than you can normally turn it, switching instructions and directions of your hands.

39

Exercise 1

Exercise 2

Exercise 3

Exercise 4

LIMBERING

40

Morehouse and Gross allot a total of one minute to performing these four limbering-up exercises. They suggest that during your first few sessions, if you hold each maximum stretch position for a few seconds, one performance of each of the movements is sufficient, even if you later want to do them two or three times each. I myself find the limbering routine so easy to take, and so rewarding with greater flexibility of my body within a week or two, that I give this portion of their ten minutes a longer allotment—say two minutes, and at least double up on everything. I still retain the ten-minute total because I chop a minute off the final segment of the program, as I'll explain when we come to it.

2. *Four minutes of muscle buildup (see page 42).* The next portion of the Morehouse-Gross program takes four minutes and concentrates on developing muscle fibers by pumping motions of your body against resistance. It involves two exercises, the first of which is the "expansion pushaway." This is like a pushup, but infinitely easier, because instead of lying on the floor and pushing your body up from it, you start by merely standing a little beyond arm's reach from a wall and, with your hands against the wall at shoulder height and your chest close to it, push away from it back to the starting position. Your heels will probably rise a bit from the floor as you do this, and that is all right, as long as you keep your legs straight, and don't bend at the knees. This ought to be pretty easy for anyone who stands quite close to the wall, but, even so, if you find that doing fifteen or twenty such pushaways is something of an exertion for you, keep at it until it

isn't. At that time move your feet farther away from the wall, and keep doing so each time you can perform more than twenty pushaways before the exertion begins to feel heavy.

The wall position may be too easy from the outset for many people. If you are one of them, use anything that lowers the height of your hands substantially below the height of your shoulders—such as a bathroom sink or a chest of drawers. At the outset you want a height that will make more than fifteen pushaways an exertion for you. At each session, as your condition improves, you'll step up the number of repetitions, and when you can do more than twenty quite easily,

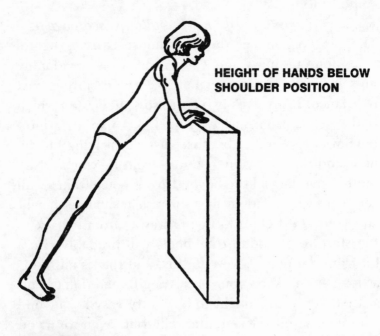

HEIGHT OF HANDS BELOW SHOULDER POSITION

PUSHAWAY

you may want to increase the difficulty by starting even lower, from a chair or bench, and possibly eventually all the way to the floor, where you will be doing push-ups rather than pushaways. But while Morehouse and Gross gradually build up a regimen well past what I'm describing here, remember that theirs is a book aimed entirely at making one physically fit, and it ranges from merely making one reasonably fit for the day's work or activity to really rigorous workouts aimed at making the truly ambitious devotee reach a physical peak. This book of mine is different. It's about playing tennis, and physical training is only a small portion of it: the goal here is no more than to wake up a body that perhaps has been allowed to grow sluggish, and get it ready to perform better on a tennis court. If you want more than that, you'll have to get their book.

The other muscle buildup exercise is the "expansion sitback," which is a much easier-to-take variation

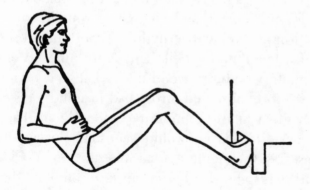

SITBACK

on the conventional situp that we all used to do in physical training in school, college, or the army. For a person who is out of condition, the situp can be all but impossible, but the sitback can be achieved by anyone to some degree. Sit on the floor and hook your feet under a piece of furniture, with your knees fully bent and your chest as close to your knees as you can get them. Then move your trunk back away from your knees until you feel your abdominal musculature come into play; you may be able to move only a few inches back or quite far back. Experiment gently at first until you find the right spot to get a mild workout. At each stage be able to hold the position for fifteen to twenty seconds: if you can't, you've moved too far and need to work back to that position in easier stages. The authors of *Total Fitness* tell you how to go well past this point, but as far as our program for you is concerned, that's enough.

3. *Five minutes of heart conditioning.* The final step to fitness that the authors of the book outline has to do with raising and measuring your heart rate to the proper level with a rhythmic, continuous exercise, over a five-minute spell. This is to build up circulo-respiratory endurance and I'm sure it's a good idea for what Morehouse and Gross had in mind—becoming truly fit. It's more complicated and arduous than most senior tennis players would want to go through if their aims aren't as noble as that and all they're trying to achieve is somewhat better physical condition that will help them cover a court more effectively than they've been able to do in recent years. The authors suggest

certain ways to get your pulse up to the proper beat for your age—their favorite is something they call "the fitness hop," running in place to music for five minutes. I myself, not being especially intent on achieving a cardiovascular training level, and finding the fitness hop not much to my liking, developed my own few minutes of steady exertion (four rather than five, as explained earlier) in the form of shadow-boxing. This not only has me dancing around the room, and twisting and turning in all directions, but also jabbing and throwing punches throughout, which gives my arms a workout as well as my legs and body.

That's as far as I ever got with the program outlined in *Total Fitness in 30 Minutes a Week.* Morehouse and Gross take their readers a very great deal further, and if you're intent on becoming a thing of exquisite physical beauty, and lessening your chances of a stroke or heart attack, and living longer, and all sorts of other admirable aims, I will repeat that you cannot do better than to get hold of a copy of that book. But if, like me, you have smaller goals, I think you have a good chance of achieving them to your considerable satisfaction by merely following the early stages of Morehouse-Gross, as given here.

All tennis players, but particularly ones of senior age, would do well to arrive ready to play a few minutes before actually going out onto the court. Five minutes, or even less, of the sort of limbering and stretching exercises you've just read about can forestall many a muscle pull or strain. Leaning against the net post and doing a few expansion pushaways will not only get your shoulders and arms ready, but will stretch the thigh and calf muscles beneficially. From the same position, you should also alternately bend one knee and then the other until your knee almost touches the ground, while at the same time extending the other leg back, on tiptoe, as far as it can go. Then, when you go out to play, particularly if the weather is cool or cold, leave on your warm-up clothing throughout the warm-up rallying period, and even for the first game or two. Under really chilly conditions, you might do well never to strip down to jersey and shorts. You can play with just about as much élan and gung-ho determination without shedding sweat clothes, and keeping warm is just about the best preventive measure you can take not to incur the minor but distressing injuries that so frequently plague tennis players.

I have used liniments and salves, such as Ben-Gay, to some good effect to try to alleviate an injury after I've suffered it, but I think the best plan is to rub it in well *beforehand* on any portion of your frame that's prone to injury. Through the years I've had a tendency now and then to pull a little muscle or ligament in the back of my knee and upper thigh if I have to start too fast and unexpectedly, as, for example, going after a well-executed drop shot that I hadn't anticipated my opponent would make. Now I never go out to play without sloshing onto this area, and rubbing in well, something like Ben-Gay. I have a friend who has incurred tennis elbow several times during his career and he is convinced that the same sort of treatment to his elbow, prior to playing, has prevented recurrences ever since he adopted the practice. Maybe we're both crazy, but as far as averting injuries is concerned, there's a lot to be said for the Power of Positive Thinking, and I recommend it to you.

Suppose you do injure yourself? What then? I am not referring to something truly ghastly, like completely rupturing your Achilles' tendon, where you yourself can't do anything, but others must do it for you—and quickly. (Off to the hospital at once and an operation within twenty-four hours and months and months at best of recuperation.) That happens, thank goodness, to very few tennis players, but we all know what it's like to sprain an ankle, or take a bruising fall, or pull a muscle—or anything that is going to put us out of action for a while. The point is: How short a period of time can you help to make it?

Today it is well known (even though, surprisingly, it wasn't in the early part of the century), that the one immediate action to take for an injury where swelling is bound to take place, which would be true of all of the above, is to apply cold, and plenty of it. A large ice pack is best and can be sustained and renewed most easily, but in a pinch a satisfactory substitute can be improvised, such as packing ice into a small leak-proof plastic bag or a rubber glove, and closing it with an elastic band. Even getting such an injury under the coldest available running water can help if no ice is available. Cold stems the swelling and enables later treatment, which can involve both heat and cold, to be much more effective.

When I incur an injury, I confess that I continue to use a liniment such as Ben-Gay, which has long been recommended, but more out of sheer desperation to do something—anything!—to enable me to get back on a tennis court as soon as possible, rather than out of a conviction that liniment heals to any extent. And all of us, including arthritis sufferers, have obtained some measure of relief from aspirin and similar products that relieve pain. Most of us, however, and this certainly includes myself, are reluctant to pop pills, even the most benign and even in small quantities. Yet today there is something comparatively new that appears to have driven all the long-established medications of the locker room out of business. No longer does a training room for athletes waft the pungent smell of liniment to the nostrils. In the words of Bill Cullen, the Princeton football team physician, no one uses the aromatic stuff any more. "Ibuprofen—Advil or something like that—that's the liniment of the nineties," Cullen says.

I've only had occasion to use ibuprofen twice, but it worked beautifully both times. Two swallows do not make a summer, but next time one of those minor injuries happens to me, I'll be trying it again (even though, admittedly, through force of habit I'll be using salves and ice packs and hot pads and everything else, because I might as well). But my hope and faith will repose in ibuprofen. Directions—and warnings (such as not to take it along with aspirin or acetaminophen)—are on the ibuprofen box that can be bought without prescription over the counter. The warnings are straightforward and neither frightening nor discouraging, even to a non-pilltaker like myself. You should take the smallest effective dose, which would probably be one or two tablets a day, and you shouldn't keep it up for more than ten days. You shouldn't combine ibuprofen with any other drugs you may be taking, and you especially shouldn't take it during the last three months of pregnancy. If you have any bad side effects, you shouldn't continue taking it at all, and you should consult your doctor.

None of that weakened my urge to give ibuprofen a second chance to pull off a miracle for me, it having done so once previously for a lesser complaint, when recently I pulled that nagging muscle or ligament or whatever it is behind my knee for the umptieth time. So I took two ibuprofen tablets a day, at least six hours apart and with meals, for less than a week. My pain had gone completely by then and I went back to play after that, albeit a little gingerly the first time, but all went well and has continued so ever since. I will add that, timid as I am about taking drugs of any sort, I consulted both my own doctor and a sports medicine consultant whom I know, before embarking on the ibuprofen treatment. Each confirmed Bill Cullen's statement, and each said that he himself used ibuprofen for the sort of pain I was experiencing.

Of course, there have always been other ways to combat pain sufficiently to allow a determined player to play. From the simple wrappings of an Ace bandage to more complex elastic bandages designed specifically for ankles, knees, thighs, forearms, wrists, and so forth, and finally to specially constructed orthopedic devices involving leather and steel, professional sports trainers and doctors have found mechanical ways to get a player who's been injured back into the game. A particularly effective device, used by many tennis elbow sufferers, is called a spider splint. Available from any surgical supply store and from some pharmacies as well, it is a simple affair that connects a leather band, pulled tightly around the upper forearm just under the elbow, to another around the wrist, by means of a rigid bar attached to each. The spider splint works so well that often someone suffering from a really painful case of tennis elbow can put one on and go out and perform at his or her best, at least for the span of the match. Statistics are not available about how the arm feels later, but from what I've seen and heard, the injury to the elbow is not aggravated by playing with a spider splint.

In any event, tennis players who are hurting slightly, but who refuse to miss their regular game, have always resorted at the very least to the elastic support, and sometimes to something much more elaborate and expensive. This is particularly true of senior players, since they are more prone to incurring such injuries, and they are likely to be the most fanatical about not missing their regular game. I should know—I'm a prime example—my purchases have supported Johnson & Johnson, Bauer & Black, and Futuro for so many years that the stockholders ought to vote me a bonus. Ben-Gay or ibuprofen or anything else aside, forsake not the elastic support when you feel one would bolster some weak point. It not only probably will, but it's a psychological comfort that helps ease you past any timidity you may have about playing. Also, the very sight of it by your opponent may give you a piece of gamesmanship to exploit (see chapter 8). This is, of course, something that the great Australian, Roy Emerson, would deplore. It was he who coined one of the best tennis philosophies ever expressed: "You should never complain about an injury. If you play, then you aren't injured, and that's that!"

Before we leave the topic of one's physical well-being, a few words might be in order about eating and drinking. I've read enough about nutrition in magazine articles and in books to think I know what a good, balanced diet is, but I'm not going to proselytize for one school of thought or another. As far as tennis players are concerned, some stars read labels carefully and pay a great deal of attention to what the medical establishment terms a healthy regimen. Other stars seem to subsist wholly on junk food. Since figures are not available about how each of these groups fares against the other, either on the tennis courts or in longevity records, I'll only tell you a few general things I believe in.

Don't overeat. It's better to leave the table a little bit hungry than to stagger away from it satiated.

Eat at least two hours before playing tennis, particularly before playing a match that's important to you, so as to give your digestion a chance to work.

Drink plenty of water throughout the day. As a matter of fact, this brings up an extraordinary reversal of medical opinion that has taken place within our lifetime: when we were young, a tennis player was not supposed to drink *any water at all* during the course of a match. If he did, the theory was that at the very least he was likely to incur a bad stitch in his side, and at the very worst, something akin to apoplexy. If you were involved in a very tough match on an excessively hot day, and your throat was literally parched, it was grudgingly conceded acceptable to take a little warm water (*never* cold!) into your mouth, gargle with it a few seconds, and then spit it out. That's all! If you allowed a few drops to trickle down your throat, you were tempting the Fates and might be destroyed!

Believe it or not—and if you are close to my age you will believe it because you'll remember it—this medical dictum held up through succeeding generations of tennis, and the genteel spitting out of water during rest periods while players changed sides was a common sight from the public courts to the sacred grounds of Wimbledon and Forest Hills.

You are undoubtedly aware that today doctors and trainers and coaches and the players themselves are unanimously agreed that the drinking of water—and lots of it—throughout a taxing match is not only permissible but close to gospel ordained from on high. I was conditioned for so many years not to drink water during a match that I'm still more sparing about gulping it down than many of my playing companions, but I'm glad to report that even the most reckless of water guzzlers don't appear to suffer any dire effects.

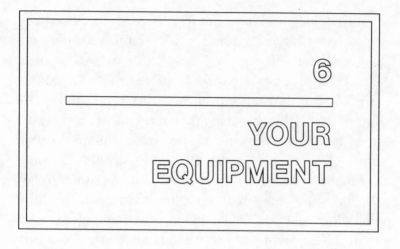

6

YOUR EQUIPMENT

If you're thinking that one of the new racquets may help your game, you may well be right, but choosing the exactly correct one out of the plethora of different racquets offered these days isn't that easy. Just to digress for a moment, there used to be a time not so many years ago when choices in life were a lot simpler. Looking to buy a new automobile, people of modest means were apt to go for a Ford, a Plymouth, or a Chevrolet. Those willing and able to spend more might ponder over Buicks, Oldsmobiles, and Chryslers. The big spenders hesitated between Packards, Lincolns, and Cadillacs.

Certainly there were other makes of cars than the nine listed above, which I picked more or less out of a hat and my casual memory, but not so many more that there was any confusion about what make of car you were buying and its general reputation. As Gertrude Stein would have put it, "A Chevrolet is a Chevrolet is a Chevrolet," and if you purchased one you got a Chevrolet—not a Chevette or a Corsica or a Celebrity or a Cavalier or a Caprice or a Cornucopia. (I made that last one up because it seemed to be appropriate for the abundance of names: all the rest really *are* Chevrolets, parading under strange monikers that don't clearly say "Chevrolet"—at least not to a non–car buff like me.) All the other car manufacturers today do the same thing without even giving you the hint that Chevrolet graciously extends by naming many of their models with words that begin with a C. But unless you really are into cars, what in the world is a Skylark, Riviera, or Regal? Or a Cutlass, Regency, or Delta? The answers, if you care, are Buicks for the first trio and Oldsmobiles for the second, but in picking these as illustrations I could just as well have cited any other car manufacturer. Quick now! Who makes the Scorpio, the Cougar, the Lynx, the Bronco, the Festive, the Ciera? Did you think I'd *never* ask?

Well, the automobile has never been either a success symbol or a sex symbol as far as I'm concerned, and I'm admittedly ignorant about the nuances of car nomenclature and uninterested in most other things concerning them. All I care about in an auto is that it runs reliably, needs only modest and very infrequent repairs, and has room in it for all four participants in a doubles match, a couple of whom are overweight. And my only purpose in bringing automobiles into this chapter at all is that a somewhat comparable situation exists with what's been going on in recent years with tennis racquets.

There was a long period in history when tennis shops carried a few choices of Spalding or Wilson or Dunlop racquets of varying prices, and that almost was that. You hefted and swung a few, found one with the weight, balance, and grip you liked, looked at the price tag, and made your selection. The chances were that if you took your tennis at all seriously, you eventually chose either a Wilson Autograph racquet (they were all pretty similar, but the one bearing the Jack Kramer signature stood out because he was the champion at the time, and over the years Wilson has had the good sense not to scrap the signature on so well established a fine racquet in favor of putting on the signature of some other more modern star), or you might have preferred a Dunlop Maxply. You never were tempted to change whichever one you bought until the frame warped or broke, or you just hankered after a new racquet, at which point you went out and got a new one as exactly like your old one as you could find. Why not? You liked the racquet you'd been using and were accustomed to its feel, and you saw that practically all of the top players, except some of the foreigners, also seemed to prefer either a Wilson Autograph or the Dunlop Maxply.

But then, along with radical new designs, head sizes, and construction materials, came new merchandising of racquets, featuring all these state-of-the-art improvements and, like cars, dubbing each slightly differing model in a line with its own individual name.

55

Now, if you look at an advertisement for a major tennis discount store, you'll find listed some twenty manufacturers offering almost two hundred different models of tennis racquets! Their prices range somewhere between three and ten times what you last paid for your trusty Jack Kramer or Maxply. And in what is surely the most exhaustive coverage and analysis of tennis racquets ever undertaken, in the March 1989 issue of *Tennis* magazine a staggering one hundred new racquets are much more than merely listed, as in the discount store's advertisement. They are pictured, described, and their merits and flaws discussed almost to the point of utter confusion. Admittedly, if you were in the market for a new racquet, you'd undoubtedly find this long article interesting and instructive, assuming you could retain the elements in it you found meaningful, while trying to grasp it all. *Tennis* did a fabulous job in covering a major aspect of the topic to which the magazine is devoted, but have racquet manufacturers' promotion and salespeople gone a little berserk? Isn't this overkill? Has it any justification or is it, to use the alternative spelling, something of a racket?

Considering how cynical I've been about the proliferation of products and names in the automobile business, it may surprise you that I'm not nearly so much so about racquets. I realize this is highly personal and unfair, since I know virtually nothing and care even less about fancy cars, while I know quite a lot and care quite considerably about tennis and tennis gear. The stretch limousine typifies to me all that is the most blatantly vulgar about modern civilization. Although I probably should, I don't have the same feeling about a $250 tennis racquet, even though I know it can't be worth that much unless it has a precious gem or two embedded in the handle. Why am I so intolerant about the one, and so much less so about the other? It's because it seems pretty clear that the differences in playing effectiveness between one racquet and another, among today's sophisticated models, can be considerable. On the other hand, if effectiveness is the consideration as opposed to ostentation, I rate a car purely on its dependable ability to transport me from point A to point B safely and as rapidly as is consistent with the speed limit.

In writing that one racquet can differ from another as far as effectiveness is concerned, I must start with a confession. For most of my tennis life, I was pretty well convinced that there really wasn't much difference, and that any experienced player—and not necessarily a high-level one—could adapt fairly quickly if he was handed a racquet quite different from the one to which he was accustomed. This unauthenticated opinion was firmed up to cast-iron strength one year when I was about 40 years old and on a visit to Bermuda. It happened that an important Bermuda tennis tournament, open to anyone who had the temerity to enter it, was scheduled to be played that week on the courts of the Bermuda Stadium in Hamilton. Since at that time I was playing as well as I ever had, and since I had no tennis-playing companion with me, I thought I'd give it a try, just to be able to get a game. I had no Walter Mitty dreams of glory, particularly when I learned that two of the British West Indies Davis Cup players were entered. All I wanted was to assure myself that I'd get in at least one match with somebody during my stay in Bermuda.

The pro at the stadium agreed, for the price of a lesson, to give me a little practice by hitting balls with me for half an hour, and I was meeting the ball pretty well against him with my trusty 13½-ounce, 4½-inch-grip Dunlop Maxply, until the moment when suddenly and unexpectedly the top of the frame snapped just as I was leaning into a serve.

The tournament was slated to start the next day. The professional had no racquet he was willing to let me use: he only had new racquets for sale. I, who had two other excellent Maxplys in good condition reposing safely in a closet back in New York, had no urge to invest in still another. However, the pro did tell me that one could rent a racquet very cheaply at Trimingham's, Bermuda's leading department store, so off I headed for Front Street. It was quite true that the store offered such a service: twenty-five cents a day for a racquet, but when I came to examine the dozen or so that were lying in a pile on the floor, I could see that twenty-five cents might be an excessive charge. There didn't seem to be a one that wouldn't be scorned by any self-respecting junkyard. Most were so warped by the Bermuda climate as to resemble a pretzel, the stringing generally seemed to have been salvaged from old fishing nets, and the wooden handles for the most part had no leather grips—some even had splinters sticking up. Finally, however, I did unearth one where the stringing seemed sound and had retained some tension, and even though it was a blunderbuss of a racquet by my lights—14¾ ounces, 4¾-inch grip, and very head-heavy—it was certainly the only faintly reasonable possibility that Trimingham's had to offer. I put down my twenty-five cents, plus a dollar for a deposit, and walked out armed with my new weapon.

It was too late to go back to the stadium that day and try it out, so the first time I could even hit one ball with it was when I faced my first-round opponent the next morning for our warm-up period. Luckily I had not drawn anyone particularly formidable, and while it took me some time to accustom myself to my rented Trimingham beauty (it didn't bear the name of any manufacturer I had ever heard of), I successfully squeezed through the first set. Then, gaining confidence by the minute, I swept through the second set handily, and by the time I met my next opponent in the second round, I had fallen in love with the racquet. I don't think I ever played better tennis than I did that week, and I won four rounds before finding myself matched against one of the B.W.I. Davis Cup players in the semifinals! The luck of the draw, in which they had been the only seeded players, had favored me up to that point, but my semifinal rival thrashed me as solidly as might be expected, ending any further pipe dreams I might have been nurturing. Still, I had played so unexpectedly well with my rented bat that I went back to Trimingham's to see if I could buy the racquet, if only as a souvenir, but they said they didn't have enough racquets to fill requests for rentals, and they needed to keep every one they had. I suppose I might simply not have gone back at all, and kept the racquet by forfeiting my dollar deposit, but I like to think I didn't do so because it wouldn't have been cricket. Privately, I have to confess I didn't think of it.

So when I got back home and picked up one of my Maxplys again, I wasn't sure what to expect, but it turned out that the switching from one racquet to a substantially different one, and then back again, neither improved my game nor caused it to suffer. I had played particularly well in Bermuda probably because the importance of the tournament challenged me, and I suppose I would have fared just as well with one of my Maxplys. I'm not at all sure, had I brought the Trimingham racquet home and used it thereafter, that the magic would have continued, but the Bermuda experience bolstered my opinion that brooding over the choice of one racquet as opposed to another is largely an exercise in the Joy of Shopping, and really doesn't prove much of anything in the end. Will Rogers claimed that he never met a man he didn't like. I used to claim that I never met a racquet in good condition that I didn't like, since one was very much like another. I continued to feel that way for years. Then, as Hollywood subtitles used to put it, Came the Dawn!

RACQUETS

My conviction began to be shaken in the mid-'70s, when I was already eligible for a senior tournament, in which I won one of the then-innovative, oversize, large-head, aluminum-frame racquets, made by Prince. With some dubious expectations I started to experiment with it one day and found that although it took a bit of getting used to, it immediately improved what was then the weakest point of my game—my volley. Clearly this was because of the larger head, not the metal frame, but that had an obvious advantage too. The Prince promotion blurbs said it added power, and maybe it did, but you couldn't prove it by me. What I did like was that the racquet didn't have to be carefully encased in one of those old-fashioned presses we all had to use to keep a wood frame from warping—always a nuisance and an actual encumbrance when packing for traveling. This new metal racquet could just be tucked away in a corner when not in use, and any time you went away, it would fit very nicely into a normal-sized suitcase along with your clothes, thus eliminating one thing to carry.

The Prince aluminum oversize racquet was the forerunner of the veritable explosion of state-of-the-arts tennis racquets that has taken place since, but even back then it was clear to me that I could no longer maintain that one racquet was pretty much like another. That first oversize head added confidence to my volley without hurting the rest of my game, once I got used to its feel. Since then, along with every other tennis player I ever heard of who made such a switch, I've never been tempted to revert to the old, conventional smaller head although, once again along with most other players, I now favor the mid-size. That's large enough to do the same good job when you're volleying, but the slightly smaller head makes the racquet more easily wielded in trying to stroke, or serve, with severity. As for that original aluminum frame, I myself never found that it added more recognizable punch to my shots than the wooden frame racquets it replaced, but later on, when aluminum was replaced by more exotic materials such as graphite, boron, and ceramic (whatever that may be—I had thought it was pottery but it obviously isn't as far as tennis racquets are concerned), by golly, it *did* make a difference. All the best players in the world were deserting their old favorites and playing with mid-size graphite or ceramic racquets, and I too found that I was hitting the ball more soundly and harder than before. (Unfortunately, so were my opponents, for the same reason!)

I now think that sort of racquet makes sense for everyone who aspires to play as good a brand of quality tennis as he is capable of, and that remark in particular would apply to anyone who is heading into the land of tennis seniors. If some of the price tags make you blink, remembering that it wasn't so terribly long ago that the best racquets cost about $25, consider the fact that it wasn't so terribly long ago that the best theater tickets to a Broadway musical cost less than $5 and a family magazine cost a quarter. At least these modern racquets are better than the old ones, which can't be said as surely about Broadway musicals or magazines. In any case, even if you can't be philosophical about the list cost of some of the top-line racquets, take heart. Things don't have to be quite as dire as they may seem. For one thing, the really fabulously priced racquets

—those listed at $200 and upward—may be just as good as those that cost half of that or less, but probably are no better. As with other products, the additional price is largely promotional hype to persuade well-heeled victims into thinking they are buying the Very Best, simply because it's the Most Expensive.

The fact is that you can buy the models of tennis racquets that the best players in the world use for around $100 in a retail tennis shop, particularly a price-competitive one, where you can see and handle what you are getting and can work up a friendly and helpful rapport with the salesperson. Alternatively, you can order your new racquet from one of the several excellent mail-order tennis discounters and save substantial money. Many of these advertise in every issue of *Tennis* and *World Tennis* magazines, and if your experience is like the ones I have had—with a firm named Holabird in Baltimore, telephone (301) 687-6400—you get lightning-like delivery and complete satisfaction.

Nor is it difficult anymore to decide what your own particular specifications should be. Everything has been greatly simplified to eliminate a number of picky option niceties that have turned out to be pretty meaningless. So you don't need to brood anymore over a racquet that weighs 12¾ ounces versus one that weighs 13 ounces—or should you go to 13⅛?—because racquets are no longer marked that way. Today they're marked L for Light, which is what most people prefer with a graphite or ceramic frame, and that's that. You can order M for Medium, and I presume H for Heavy if you're so minded, but I don't know anybody who has ever gone for an H, and I wouldn't advise a senior player to look for anything other than L.

What else needs to be considered? The size of your grip, certainly, and that's one of the things you specify when ordering from a mail order house. If you've been playing tennis for any length of time, you doubtless know what size grip suits you, but if you are not sure, here's a way of checking matters remarkably accurately. Measure with a ruler the distance from the middle crease of your hand (the one that runs almost laterally across the center of the palm) to the tip of your ring finger (the one next to the pinkie). Measure accurately to the nearest eighth of an inch and you'll have your proper grip size. Men usually run between 4½ and 4¾ inches, women between 4⅛ and 4⅜.

You may think that the tension of the stringing is a most important consideration for you to determine, particularly if you've read some very confusing things about string tension. Björn Borg had his racquets strung extremely tightly: more than 80 pounds pressure per inch, while John McEnroe prefers what most stringers would deem a very loosely strung racquet—less than 50 pounds pressure. The modern theory about these variations is just the opposite of what it used to be, and just the opposite of what would seem to be common sense. It was once thought that the tighter the stringing, the more powerful the shot would be, while the looser, the more "touch" could be exerted on a ball. I still think that's logical, but modern tennis intelligentsia say nay. They maintain that the tight stringing is for better control and the looser stringing for more power. Are you confused enough not to know what to do? My advice is to forget both Borg and McEnroe, each a genius who at his best could beat the rest of the world even if Borg used a loosely strung bat and McEnroe a tightly strung one, and just accept the stringing tension recommended by the manufacturer of the model you're ordering. It will undoubtedly be between the mid-50s and the mid-60s, and it really doesn't matter exactly at what point within that range it happens to fall. Somewhere around there has always been considered about right for most players, from the ordinary to champions. Accepting the manufacturer's recommendation is as practical a compromise solution to the Borg-McEnroe perplexity as you're likely to find.

Gut or nylon stringing? Top-grade gut is very marginally superior in its playing qualities and, if you have serious tournament aspirations, and if you don't mind paying not only the original cost of gut but the inevitable replacement cost when your strings break every now and then, by all means choose gut. Under any other circumstances, I don't think there's much doubt that you should go for good-quality nylon. Very few weekend players, even very good ones, can tell the difference, and play just as well with nylon stringing as with gut. Nylon's advantages are first, of course, its lower price, and second, its durability. Nylon not only doesn't fray the way gut does, it isn't affected adversely by dampness or even real wetness. Using a modern racquet having a graphite or ceramic frame, and strung with nylon, allows you to play right through a light shower with complete lack of concern. I'm sure our British tennis friends, who are likely to encounter that situation almost every time they go out to play, must be very grateful for nylon.

In the few years since the wonderful new frames have sprung up in such staggering numbers, I've tried out quite a few and eventually liked them all, sometimes immediately and sometimes after a short while. The racquet I love best is invariably the one I secured last and am using currently, and it would be bootless for me to recommend one over the other except in the most general terms. A racquet's "feel" should count more with you than an impressive label, a celebrity's endorsement, its cosmetic appeal, or a seductive carrying case. "Feel" is usually a matter of what sort of balanced weight pleases you when you swing a racquet—an even balance, a heavy head, or a light one, a comfortable grip. You may well fancy one of the new "widebody" frames: there are those who swear by them, and no less an authority than Gene Scott has predicted that it's only a question of time before all other types of racquet become obsolete. Wilson started it all with its Profile racquet, and got a patent on it, but now all the other racquet manufacturers get around that by making their widebodies not quite so wide. They can thus claim, with some credibility, that their racquets may not be quite so powerful as Wilson's Profile, but they make it easier to control the ball. So in order to be all things to all players, Wilson now also produces a not-quite-so-wide-as-the-Profile bat in addition to the original Profile.

Visit the shop with the biggest variety of racquets

in your area and swing a few that appeal to you, trying forehand, backhand, and service motions. You may get enough of a feel there and then to decide on one or another, but if not, many of the more enterprising tennis shops will allow you to take a floor-sample racquet away and play with it, charging you a daily rental fee for the privilege of trying it out. Then, if you like the racquet, the rental fee counts toward the purchase of a new one. Or you may smile pleasantly as you return the rental racquet, indicate that you haven't made up your mind, and forfeit the rental fee. The truth is that you like the racquet very much and you're going to telephone an order for one to your mail order discount house. If you play only a couple of times a week, it will probably arrive, professionally strung, so quickly that you may not even miss one session before you can use it. And if you think there's something not quite cricket about all this, know that the retail shop has become so accustomed to people doing this that they make their one-day rental sufficiently high that it's not a bad business in itself. As far as your own economics are concerned, you will save enough buying from the discounter to pay the forfeited rental fee many times over.

SHOES

The next most important thing in tennis equipment is shoes, but there's not too much to say on that score.

We all grew up wearing sneakers perfectly happily on tennis courts, but that word now appears to be all but obsolete, and the modest footwear it denoted almost equally so. Today there is nothing but "tennis shoes," and if you want to buy a pair of sneakers to wear on the beach, or to putter around in the garden, or (heaven forbid!) to play tennis in, you'd be rather hard put to find a place that sells them—except for children. Children can still be sold sneakers in places like Woolworth's or Lamston's, but anybody claiming to be a tennis player must wear "tennis shoes." Admittedly any bitterness in the last sentence is essentially a matter of nomenclature: I resent the fact that a perfectly fine and familiar friend, the word "sneaker," has been expunged from the language in favor of "tennis shoe."

To be more fair about it, the modern tennis shoe does indeed have it all over the old sneaker, as it jolly well should, since it costs almost ten times as much. I'm not sure you can play any better in them, but the big thing is that your feet will stand up better. Today's tennis shoe is scientifically contoured and cushioned and ventilated and whatnot, and—particularly for a senior player, whose arches may not be what they once were—it makes sense to shoot the works and go for a pair of shoes that truly suit your feet. You're certainly going to have plenty of choices. The tennis shoe industry is far larger than the racquet industry, at least in dollar volume ($650 million as opposed to $135 million), and this is not too surprising, since tennis racquets are used only for playing tennis, while tennis shoes are the footwear of choice of the entire world:

concertgoers, cat burglars, office staffs, Romeos and Juliets. While the variety of models in shoes may not match the mind-boggling number of racquets that exist, the proliferation of styles and models in tennis footwear is pretty staggering too. Nike alone has twenty-four different categories. (The figures quoted above come from the 1989 sports goods Super Show, which is now put on annually at Atlanta's World Congress Center, as reported by Eugene L. Scott in the February 23, 1989 issue of *Tennis Week*.)

If you want to buy a pair of tennis shoes of a brand you've never tried before, go to a good shop, where you will be fitted properly. Once you're happy with a model, and know the exact size and width that fits your foot, you may want to order subsequent pairs from a mail-order discounter where, in percentage terms, once again substantial savings can be obtained. However, even though tennis shoes of reputation are expensive, they are not in the same league with what racquets cost, and the actual money savings may not seem worthwhile. Also, between one pair of shoes and a new pair, your feet may have changed in one way or another sufficiently for a new fitting to be wise. In any event, the best shoes for your particular feet are a good investment for any tennis player, but especially for one who hopes to enjoy playing quality tennis after 50 . . . or 60 . . . or 70. . . . You can stagger along more or less well with almost any moderately decent tennis racquet, but if your feet give out, you're a gone goose. Incidentally, if despite having good shoes, you tend to develop blisters on your feet while playing, try wearing two pairs of socks. Two pairs of any type will probably do the trick, but the best combination is a lightweight pair worn next to the skin, with a heavier woolen pair pulled over them.

OTHER CLOTHING AND ACCESSORIES

We now come to a tennis topic that has very little, if anything, to do with the actual playing of the game of tennis, but which looms very large in certain social circles, and is at least interesting for anyone who plays the game regularly. It also adds flavor for spectators, watching a big field of players in a tournament. The topic is a fashion one—who is wearing what?

The historical tradition calls for "tennis whites," an all-white costume from shirts and shorts down to socks and shoes. No color at all is allowed except a grudging concession granted to the least garish of trims on collars, or a modest stripe on the pocket of shorts or the top of socks. There are certain estimable private clubs who observe this tradition so reverently that they insist on all-whites as a regular daily thing for their members and guests of both sexes, no matter how informal a game. (In some cases, the club's shop can make a good thing out of selling new gear to guests who are unaware of the regulations and arrive decked out in the gaudy colored outfits they are accustomed to wear!) Such clubs have to let down the bars about color outfits when the professionals play at them, because they know that pros have contractual obligations to wear their sponsors' products, which at the very least involve a commercial logo with color. Men professionals, for the most part, stick to white shorts, but many prefer fairly gaudy shirts. The majority of the women professionals seem to favor white, but there are many who wear stunning colored tennis dresses, usually pastels, and even the stuffiest and most conservative old-line club is not likely to dictate to professionals of either sex what they can and cannot wear. Not if it wants them to play in its tournaments and attract the crowds—and it does, it does.

But let's get back to what matters as far as playing tennis is concerned. Does Ivan Lendl serve more aces as the result of the variegated color designs on his jersey? Did Chris Evert punch her wonderful two-handed backhand so unerringly down the line past her opponent partly because her pink tennis dress was so pretty? I think not. The only things that would matter to them, as far as playing effectiveness is concerned, would be that their clothes were neither so tight that they bound, nor so loose that they flapped annoyingly. So from that standpoint, what one wears on a tennis court isn't that significant.

In other ways it may be, however. For myself, as a spectator, I am invariably pleased to attend an event that calls for all-whites, such as the Wimbledon championships, particularly when the tournament is played on grass courts, but then I have a strong sentimental streak. However, I possess only two sets of all-whites, simply so I can play at places that insist on that costume: this doesn't happen often enough for me to need more than two sets. Otherwise I wear a variety of colored shirts and shorts for three reasons: (1) I like color; (2) since people never know what to give a man for Christmas or his birthday, I get my share as gifts; and (3) I can wear color gear more than once without having to send it to the laundry to look presentable, and this is convenient, particularly when I'm on vacation.

So the choice of playing outfits is usually no big deal, and somebody playing in the T-shirt he inherited from his Uncle Harry and a pair of cut-off blue jeans (Andre Agassi fans, ahoy!) is every bit on an even footing against an opponent sporting the most splendiferous—and expensive—outfit that any Italian designer can come up with.

With outer tennis clothing, we come to still another comparatively modern production—the tennis warm-up suit. As long as I can buy one I like, I'm all for the warm-up suit, even though it really is no more practical than the old gray sweatshirt and sweatpants I had back in high school. Its virtue is that it looks nice going to and resting between sets on a cool day, and returning home from a tennis date with a possible stopover for refreshments along the way. My trouble is that it's almost impossible to find a warm-up suit that isn't plastered all over with a large commercial logo or letters spelling out the name of some fashionable tennis couturier. For all I know you may be one of those people who actually *like* to strut around advertising the fact that you're wearing a well-known and expensive brand of clothing, but to add one more piece of cantankerousness to this confessedly opinionated book, that turns me off so completely that I'd rather dig the old sweatshirt and pants out of the closet. Still, what do you care about my foibles? Nothing, nor should you. So go get yourself a warm-up suit that you like, garish or not, as long as it keeps you *warm*. To keep from getting chilled and stiff after a tough match is a good idea for any tennis player of any age, but it's a must for the senior player, who needs to keep warm for an additional reason. As we grow older, but continue to scamper as hard as we can around a tennis court, we are more susceptible to muscle pulls and strains than we once were. Keeping your muscles warm, possibly even through an entire match if the weather is on the cold side, is sound practice, particularly if you are at all nervously nursing a healing muscle injury.

These days, even the most idiotically fancy warm-up suit is at least tailored to be practical during vigorous play, and it does make you look as if you might be a good tennis player more than Uncle Harry's old T-shirt does. Remember what Polonius told Laertes in *Hamlet* about buying good clothes—"the apparel oft proclaims the man." I'm afraid Polonius was something of a boob, but his advice may be good as far as warm-up suits for senior players is concerned. If you look like a good player, it may have an intimidating effect on your opponent. (There will be more about this and related matters a bit later, when we take up the subject of gamesmanship.)

Well, as long as we're in the tennis shop, what else is likely to attract us 50-plus oldsters or, for that matter, what else is likely to be thrust upon us? One thing would surely be headgear of some sort, for regardless of what else may be involved, most tennis players—particularly those who wear glasses—want to have something to keep sweat from running down into their eyes. The simplest and cheapest device, which for most people is as good as any other, is no more than a terrycloth sweatband of whatever width and color that pleases you. A splendid tennis appurtenance is the felt visor, which has an extremely absorbent sweatband in addition to the visor aspect, which helps shield the eyes from the sun. I don't think you can beat this visor for getting the most benefit from a piece of sports headgear—unless you're bald, in which case a cap or hat might be advisable. The visor first appeared as the unique trademark of the great Helen Wills in the 1920s and '30s. No one else wore it then, and very few tennis top-notchers have taken to it since; instead, a remarkable number of professional golfers have. As I recall, it was Arnold Palmer who started the rage among tournament golfers and it continues with them, but you will look long and hard before encountering a major tennis star who sports what was once known as "the Helen Wills visor." I don't know why.

However, many journeymen tennis players, myself included, like to wear a visor to soak up perspiration and to cut down the sun's glare. An over-50 player may well find it a boon, particularly if he wears glasses and even more particularly if he's threatened with developing cataracts, but isn't yet ready for surgery. The visor shields the eyes from the light rays that make seeing the ball and the lines on the court difficult when one has partial cataracts. A baseball cap with a longish visor embodies these advantages too, and adds an extra one for the player on the bald side by covering the Achilles' heel on the top of the skull, but a cap usually doesn't have the thick sweatband that's a feature of the best grade of the Helen Wills type of visor. Of course, Helen Wills wasn't bald.

On the subject of sweat, what about wristbands? Buying and using them is up to you. Almost all big-time players do wear them, and clearly if perspiration forms on your forearms and runs down your wrists onto the palm of your hand, a wristband on your racquet arm is a blessing. Wearing one on the other wrist as well, which is what most wristband wearers seem to do, could have three possible explanations. The first, and most logical, is that the wearer is a two-handed tennis player. The second is that he wants to be sure of a dry palm on the ball toss for a serve. The third, and perhaps most likely, is that they're sold in pairs, so why not use both?

I don't have forearm sweat problems of this sort, and so have never felt the need to wear wristbands. These days, playing doubles for the most part, and so not too often having to run myself ragged, I need them even less. However, the palm of my racquet hand does sweat profusely and, as a result, I've become an advocate of the tennis glove. I first bought one when I was playing tennis at a club in the tropics, where the racquet kept slipping out of my hand. The glove seemed wonderful to me, and later I continued to find it a comfort, even in cooler weather. Today I rely on having a tennis glove just about as much as any other extra tennis gear I may use. There are only two problems concerning gloves. They become stiff and unserviceable, or they wear out, fairly quickly. And when you go to buy a new one, for some reason shops invariably (and infuriatingly) seem to be stocked with nothing but "Ladies', Left Hand." This is one of life's unfathomable mysteries, but it's taught me a lesson. Whenever I encounter a display of "Men's, Right Hand" gloves, I buy two or three of them, whether I need them right away or not.

Finally, if you are one of those lucky people who can wear sunglasses and actually see the flight of the ball and everything else on the court as well as if you weren't wearing them, bless you. I know there are those who can wear them, although I can't recall any top-notchers who did except, possibly, the old-time Czech hero, Jaroslav Drobny, who won Wimbledon in 1954, and I've only a hazy memory that he did. However, in less exalted circles, I've seen and played with quite a few good weekend players who wore dark glasses, especially when serving into the sun, so it's obvious that some can do it. I wish I were one of them—but I have lots of tennis wishes, such as being able to hit a forehand like Ivan Lendl. So much for wishes.

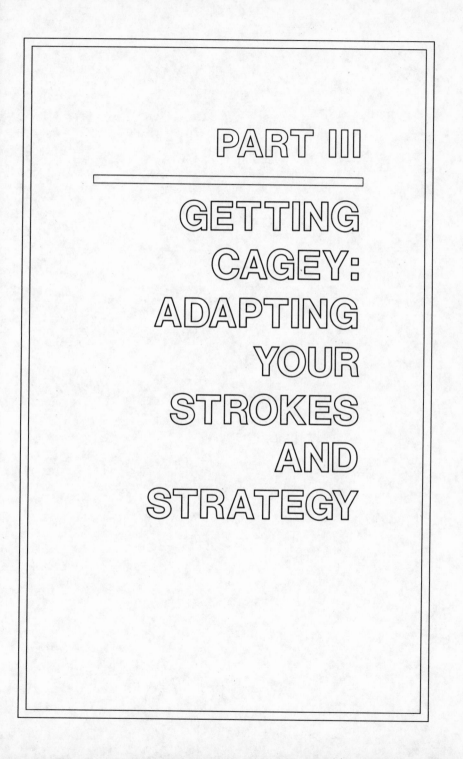

PART III

GETTING CAGEY: ADAPTING YOUR STROKES AND STRATEGY

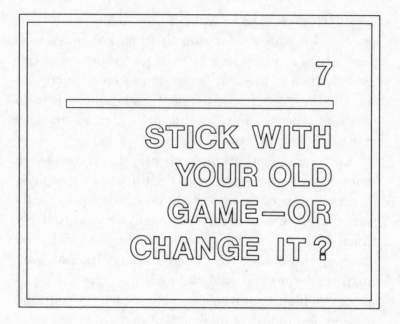

7

STICK WITH YOUR OLD GAME—OR CHANGE IT ?

With the possible exception of cookbooks, it's doubtful that any category of book resembles one another more than tennis instruction books. How many times have we read about shaking hands with the racquet in order to obtain the correct forehand grip, about turning one's side to the net while stroking on either the forehand or backhand flank, about punching volleys, about concentrating and watching the flight of the ball all the way onto the strings of one's racquet, et cetera, et cetera? Here is where this tennis book you're reading departs from the ranks. Its author presumes you're already aware of all these tennis truisms, so this paragraph contains the first, and just about the last mention

79

they'll receive. There will be one exception to this resolve. For the very reason that you are an over-50 player, you're going to gear your game somewhat differently than in the past, so we have to look at certain accepted-as-gospel instructional techniques, just to question whether they're still applicable to the way you can best play now.

Let's assume, as we probably can, that you're aware that you no longer have quite the up-and-at-'em physical competence you once had, though the spirit hasn't waned at all. Even when you are only 50 you are likely to have lost an edge off your body abilities, and at 60 or older you almost surely have. To compensate you might make several adaptations in your former techniques, which could bolster your efforts to continue playing and enjoying quality tennis.

The first and truly basic change is the way you ought to think about how you intend to hit the ball from now on. Even if your stroking always was rather smooth, try now to make it even more fluid. Keep all your forceful shots, from your serve through your drives to your net play, simple and natural, with no waste motion or useless effort. What matters is the actual hitting of the ball itself, and all the frantic and jerky energy that tennis players exert with arms and shoulders and wrists doesn't mean a thing. It has always been true that the best players let the racquet do the work, and that's particularly true of how you should be thinking today. If you concentrate on stroking gracefully with *controlled* power, letting the racquet do the job for which it was so carefully constructed, you'll obviously not wear yourself out the way you would if you were trying to pound every ball. Stamina is something every older player has to consider. The ability to "let the racquet do the work" is easier now, when all the modern state-of-the-art racquets yield so much more power for the same effort. That's particularly true of the new widebody racquets, so the next time you're in the market for a new bat, consider renting a widebody and try it out for a while. Those I know who have adopted it say it takes a bit of getting used to, and some maintain that it's actually too much racquet and one loses control, but others claim that once you get the feel of it, nothing can compare with it for the power it imparts without much help from you. That might make it the ideal model for a well-over-50 player. I intend to try one the next time I'm in the market for a new racquet.

Tactics and strategy can be every bit as important as strokes, when two well-matched veterans face each other in a singles match. Whenever you get involved in such an encounter, there is one aspect that you might not have considered. Your tactics should vary widely if one of you is in considerably better shape than the other.

Let's say that you are in better condition than your opponent. In that case, it's a wise tactic to serve wide on the great majority of your service points—to his forehand in the deuce court and to his backhand in the ad court (assuming he is right-handed, but the same principle applies if he is left-handed—serve wide). Such serves will draw him steps out of court each time, which should give you a substantial advantage, assuming you can follow up with your next shot and shoot his return of your serve off toward the other corner. You should try running him corner to corner alternately as long as the point continues; if he's out of shape, he's going to get mighty tired of it after a while. Occasionally, you might see that he's trying so desperately to get from one corner to the other that you'll steer the ball back to the corner from which he's running, thus "wrong-footing" him. But on the whole, your strategy is to run him from corner to corner as often as you can, and not just on your service games but on his too, because he's going to drop before you will.

Conversely, if *he* has the edge on *you* physically, and you are the one likely to poop out first, not only serve most of the time down the middle, near the center line, but also hit your subsequent shots generally into the center of the court, as deep as you safely can. That not only reduces your chances of making errors, because you won't often be shooting for the sidelines, but it tends to make your opponent's returns come back to you in the central portion of the court. If he does angle a shot toward your sideline, you can reach it a lot more easily than if you had hit a shot to one of his corners, and he had answered with a drive back to your court up your sideline. So the tactic of playing for the most part down the center is a good one for you, if you tire more easily than your rival; while it makes him run less, it does the same for you. That tends to diminish the physical gap between you, which would otherwise give him an edge.

Do note that in advocating these tactics I have used phrases like "on the whole" and "most of the time," because no tennis player should cleave 100 percent to a general plan of shot-making. You have to mix things up with enough variety that your opponent doesn't get into a happy groove of knowing just where and how a ball is going to come to him next. So what do I mean by "on the whole" and "most of the time"? At least 80 percent of the time.

Another aspect of tactics also has to do with physical condition, but it involves you alone and your evaluation of your capacity to play the best tennis you can at this stage of your life. Think about this: Should you stick to the fundamental type of play you've always favored or, advancing age now becoming a factor, might you be inclined—or advised—to change it radically?

Let's say you've always been a model of steadiness and consistency. You've regularly run down virtually any shot your opponents threw at you, and you've made incredible returns off shots that seemed to have you beaten. You've been a pretty consistent winner through the years because most of your opponents committed an error before you did. But as time goes by, you're beginning to find that you're not quite so gung-ho about chasing down every apparently irretrievable shot to a corner and getting it back. Dammit—you're now 55 (or 65 or 75), and your legs and your wind and possibly your common sense are beginning to protest.

On the other hand, you now have a wonderful new graphite or ceramic mid-size racquet—possibly even a widebody—that's been enabling you to hit a ball harder more consistently than you ever were able to do before. For the most part, you've found this out when rallying: once a real match has started, and there's a score to be kept, your defensive instinct to keep the ball in play, and not make unforced errors, has deterred you from throwing caution to the winds and hitting out. Let's pause a moment and think about it: How does the idea strike you of taking more chances in the future, going for outright winners whenever you have an opening, and getting points over with *fast*? True, you're going to lose some matches that you would have won playing your old way, but you might win some too against rivals who could beat you before. The real point is that shooting the works, and either winning or losing points in jig time rather than in interminably long exchanges, would be infinitely less exhausting, and it also might be much more fun. Mightn't it?

Maybe.

Then there's the diametrically opposite situation in which you've been a believer, and an exponent of the Big Game. You've been going in on your serve and storming the net at every opportunity, and you've scorned playing it safe. But perhaps your body and your eyesight aren't up to it anymore and you'd be more effective staying back, keeping the ball in play, and in general playing a baseline game. After all, if you still have the urge to be aggressive and swat the ball, you can do so from the rear of the court by mastering topspin on your drives, which is not that hard to learn. Knowing how to apply topspin will allow you the satisfaction of banging the bejabbers out of a ball, sending it with good clearance over the net but having it fall safely in court before it reaches the baseline. So what about it? Is it possibly time to discard the Big Game with the extreme exertion that net rushing demands, and become a less flashy but more consistent performer?

Maybe.

There's no one who can choose between those two "maybes" except you. Habit is an understandably strong factor in such a decision, and the chances are that most older players will continue to play the sort of game they always favored, but if one's physical circumstances have changed as a result of getting older, it's worth at least thinking about whether a change might be beneficial—and might be fun.

An elderly former tennis pro named Jack Barnaby recently wrote an amusing piece for *Tennis Week* that presented a truly original thought about how oldsters can win by turning their former orthodox thinking, particularly about serving, topsy-turvy. His theory was that very few older players possessed severe and devastating services anymore—that they more or less wafted their serves into play. No one is too likely to ace you in senior play, nor are you likely to score many aces. So being the server when you're a veteran doesn't carry the very considerable advantage that it generally is recognized as having in tennis. Since that is true of both your opponent and you, what possible advantage can you make out of it?

Barnaby's answer was to concentrate on winning

the games *when one is receiving*. Returning a serve that isn't really an aggressive weapon at all is just about the easiest shot in the world to let you take the offensive. So punish an opponent's weak serve that comes right at you at a pace that makes it seem like batting practice, and win a bunch of games when you're receiving, and hope and try for the best when you take up the challenge of serving. Even if you can't ace a rival with speed of delivery, learn to put your first serve in as often as possible *with spin*—a slice is the easiest and most effective spin service in anyone's arsenal, and you'll win some share of your service games too. So if you can manage to win a majority of games when you receive, you'll be home free. Barnaby did just that, won a 75-and-over event, and has a plaque to prove it.

He didn't point out in his article that it would be logical to choose to receive if you win the spin of the racquet to decide how a match will start. If you win the first game when your opponent is serving, it could easily upset him enough to help you win the second game too, when you're on serve. I can think of another piece of evidence that tends to substantiate the concept. Watch women's tennis—even top-notch women's tennis. These players don't patball their serves by any means, but they don't overpower their opponents on serve either, as happens so often in men's top-level tennis. The result is that serves are broken regularly in the women's game, and you always have to be nervous about your favorite woman player holding her serve, when she seems to have a set or a match in hand.

We'll have some more aspects of strategy that the older tennis player might well think about when we come to the next section, which will be devoted to the game of doubles. Right now, however, and for almost the only time in this book, let's ponder whether the older player should consider any changes in stroke production as well. On the whole, a tennis player with years of experience behind him is not too likely to change the way he approaches and hits the ball, although he may wish he could do it a little better. Habit and muscle memory are probably too ingrained to make it possible to teach an old dog many new tricks, even assuming it's desirable, which is a debatable assumption. That is why there is comparatively little discussion in this book about changing stroke techniques radically, but there are three variations on orthodox methods that you might possibly find of value.

The first is to practice a slice serve over and over again, until you have confidence that you can put it into the service boxes on both sides, placed deep and pretty near where you want it to go, a substantial percentage of the time. If you've been a pretty good player, this has been your most frequent second serve because, with the spin the slice imparts, you can hit it fairly briskly and it still won't carry out. On your first serve, you've been trying to do much more than that, hoping to take over control of a point with a hard serve and even score a few aces.

That's the way to play tennis when you're young. Now that you're older (and wiser), practice and get so adept with that old slice second serve that you can use it as an effective first serve as well. If you can put a good slice serve, even if it's of medium pace, into the service box two-thirds of the time or better, you're going to win a lot of matches in senior tennis. You'll practically never double fault, and you'll drive certain opponents crazy, for a majority of tennis players find that playing against hard-hitting is a lot easier than pacing one's strokes effectively when encountering spin. One has to think about how you return a slice or chop to best effect, whereas meeting a flat serve or drive fits the pattern of play to which one is generally accustomed. It's doing what comes naturally, whereas lunging at the erratic bounce of a spin can be intimidating.

The second variation is the two-handed backhand, a stroke that was not unknown in long bygone years (viz. John Bromwich and Pancho Segura), but which was employed by no more than a handful of recognized star players of either sex. In recent times, however, it has been adopted with notable success by a great many. Although a lot of the men use the two-handed backhand, an even greater percentage of the women do, and junior players of both sexes are inclined to favor the stroke over the traditional one-hander. With apologies to obvious he-men who do so, like Jimmy Connors, it might appear that the two-handed backhand has an appeal for those who may not be quite strong enough to hit the orthodox one-hander with any real power. This is certainly true of young children, and it's logical to think it could also be true of players who are getting on in years. For one thing, they may have developed tennis elbow by hitting the one-handed backhand a little faultily, or too frequently. That is one of the prime explanations given as a cause for some tennis elbow cases, and shifting to the two-handed backhand is a prescription often advised. For another thing, it's natural that one's physical strength and energy may have waned to some extent—not in one's 50s I would hope, but at some later time—and the easier, reinforced way of returning a backhand with two hands is a relief. There is supposed to be a disadvantage to using it in that one can't stretch for the far-out ball as effectively. Well, maybe one can't, but you'd never know it watching old-timers like Chris Evert and Jimmy Connors, or newcomers like Arantxa Sanchez-Vicario and Michael Chang, to say nothing of dozens of other luminaries, who have no more trouble than anyone else reaching the ball on their backhands. So if you are not hitting your backhand as well as you once did, or if you never did hit it particularly well, you might experiment with the two-hander. It's not a hard shot to learn, since it's close to the same grip and stroke with your racquet hand that you've always used, but now it's merely backed up and strengthened by the reinforcement of the other hand.

The third variation in stroke technique that you might want to contemplate is one that a virtually unknown tennis pro named Dick Bradlee tried to introduce more than twenty years ago. He had an idea about preparing to make a stroke that went counter to all traditional tennis teaching. The result was that when he wrote a short book entitled *Instant Tennis* outlining his theories, no major publisher was inclined to take on a treatise so revolutionary that the tennis establishment would almost surely either denigrate it or ignore it. Finally a minor book publisher, who was a tennis player himself, was sufficiently impressed to take a chance and issue a small printing in paperback form. It was a flop and soon went out of print; to try to procure a copy today would be a bootless task. I know—I tried.

Well, I think that poor old Dick Bradlee may have been a prophet before his time. For in this era, dominated by hard-surface courts both indoors and outdoors, where the receiver of a ball gets such a quick and often skiddy bounce, you will see Bradlee's basic methods being used all the time by the world's best players, whether they ever heard of Bradlee or not. If one of them is up against a powerful server, like Lendl, on a fast-surface court, he simply has no time to step across in one direction or the other, so as to turn his side to the net in approved closed-stance textbook fashion, in order to make his stroke. No—he either blocks the ball from quite an open stance or, if he can, takes at most a quick short step forward with his lead foot in order to make a more forceful return, but he still does it from a comparatively open stance.

Heresy! Blasphemy! That whirring noise you hear is the bodies of ancient great tennis teachers spinning around in their graves! But the fact is that a number of wonderful bygone stars often did the same thing when playing on what was, back then, the fastest surface—grass. Look at some of the photographs of Fred Perry, the British star who dominated world tennis in 1934, 1935, and 1936, if you require proof. I doubt whether Perry consciously meant to be unorthodox, but he was such a good natural athlete that when lightning reflexes were called for, he didn't disdain hitting from an open stance, even though his form was generally conventional and extremely stylish. There were others too, but Perry is the person who comes first to mind.

Today there are many fewer grass courts than back then, but most tennis, both professional and amateur, is now being played on surfaces that are equally fast or even faster, and the sight of shots being hit from an open stance, especially on receiving service, has become commonplace.

Bradlee maintained that hitting from an open stance was a good idea basically, whether the surface was fast or not. Even though some considered him a kind of nut case, Bradlee stuck to his guns and preached his message to anybody who would listen. He claimed that hitting a tennis ball should not involve the complications in form that the teaching professionals and tennis instructional literature insisted on. He maintained that it should all be just as simple as the natural athletic motion of throwing a ball. That is, if you're right-handed, you pivot your body by turning your shoulders and hips to the right and then, as your arm goes along and extends in back of you, take a step forward with your left foot, landing on it just as your arm comes through with the throw. (Opposite directions apply, of course, if you're left-handed.) Translating that to a tennis stroke, you should face your opponent squarely

91

at first, not knowing to which side of you he is going to hit the ball. The moment you (a right-hander) see it coming to your forehand, you start the shoulders/hips pivot to the right as you move toward it, which gives you the benefit of early racquet preparation, an absolute necessity on a fast court. As the ball bounces in front of you, you take your step forward to meet it and to hit it. That's all. There's no need for the fancy bit of turning your side to the net, which means there's also no need to recover from that position and scurry to get back and ready for the next shot. You have never stopped being ready.

On the backhand, it's the same thing in reverse. As the ball starts to come to you on that side, pivot your shoulders and hips to the left, wait for the bounce, and get your weight into the shot by taking a step forward with your right foot as you make the stroke. (Yes, you can do it equally well with a two-handed backhand if that has been your shot, or if you're thinking of converting to being a two-hander on that side.) The motion on the backhand obviously can't be compared to the throwing of a ball, but it's very similar to an equally natural athletic motion, the scaling of a Frisbee.

Simple? Yes, indeed. Bradlee called his concept "instant" tennis because it could be learned and used so readily by anybody who could throw a ball, without the complexities of traditional body positions, footwork, and so forth. I think he had something back then that the establishment refused to consider, and I suspect that if Bradlee were still around today to push his theory, he would find more of an open door for it than he did twenty years ago. I don't claim it's holy writ, and it may not be anything that Andre Agassi or Steffi Graf need think about, but an over-50 player—particularly one who is finding court coverage more of a problem than it once was—might well want to experiment with Bradlee's brainstorm. I have found it helpful, particularly in hitting a forehand, where I can exert just as much power from an open stance as from a closed one. On the backhand, I confess that you can get more of a punch into a drive from a closed stance, but if you haven't time to get into that position, you can make a perfectly fine backhand shot from the open stance as well, especially if your basic backhand stroke is a slice. It's only on the flat or topspin backhand drive that a closed stance gives one an advantage.

It may be that you're already hitting the ball from a more or less open stance without being fully conscious of it. Many journeymen tennis players do. However, if you're not conscious of it, you are not taking full opportunity to do a good job, because you'll just be standing there, facing the net and simply meeting the ball as it comes near you as best you can. If you're not conscious of it, you are not pivoting your shoulders and hips, and getting your racquet back in the early racquet preparation position, set to uncoil from the pivot and take that forward step as you swing into the shot. There's just as much *thought* involved as if you were concentrating on turning your side to the net in textbook fashion, but there isn't nearly as much exertion and work. What's more, you're going to be bet-

93

ter positioned for the next shot that your opponent will be directing toward you—provided he can handle yours.

Bradlee's system is pretty much the way good net players handle themselves for volleys. The pivot and the arm extension to the rear are very much reduced, but the idea is the same. I don't recall what he wrote about it in his book, but I'd assume that even Dick Bradlee would concede that one ought to turn one's side to the net when serving, and when hitting an overhead.

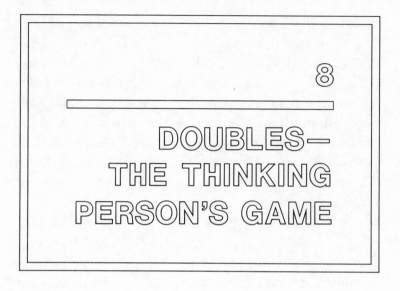

8

DOUBLES—
THE THINKING
PERSON'S GAME

It is now time to turn to the subject that is likeliest to be of the greatest interest to the senior tennis player. Most of us start out playing singles and more or less shun doubles for a long time, but inevitably—perhaps not at fifty but almost surely ten or fifteen years later—we turn to doubles, and we find it's a different and in many ways a more intriguing game than singles. That is, we do unless we were lucky enough and perceptive enough to have discovered the fact a long time before.

History shows that a great many of the world's best singles players can also be numbered among the world's best doubles players, which isn't much of a surprise. Maybe almost all great singles players could have been equally great at doubles if they had chosen to compete at that form of tennis. A great many never did, at least not seriously, but among the men Bill Tilden, Adrian Quist, Henri Cochet, Jack Kramer, Rod Laver, and John McEnroe are outstanding examples of singles champions who also scored prominently in major doubles competition. The same is true when one looks at women's records: Suzanne Lenglen, Alice Marble, Louise Brough, Margaret Osborne, Margaret Smith Court, and Martina Navratilova come to mind immediately.

More interesting are the tennis players of both sexes who, while they obviously could hold their own much of the time on a singles court, were positive geniuses at doubles, and could team and win with any of a number of partners. Among the men, such players were Jacques Brugnon, John Bromwich, George Lott, and Roy Emerson. (Emerson won the French doubles championship over six consecutive years, 1960–1965, with five different partners! Cochet, René Lacoste, and Jean Borotra were the flashy singles players on France's unbeatable Davis Cup team of the Four Musketeers in the 1930s, but the fourth member, Jacques Brugnon, was a more effective teammate in doubles for any of them than any two of them were for each other. John Bromwich of Australia and George Lott of the United States seemed to be able to pair up with any compatriot and sweep the doubles field in their respective days.)

Then there have been partnerships that concentrated on doubles, and regularly brushed aside teams composed of two very considerably more successful singles players than they. Examples from the past might be Bob Hewitt and Frew McMillan, Bob Lutz and Stan Smith, and Gardnar Mulloy and Billy Talbert, while these days Ken Flach and Robert Seguso and Rick Leach and Jim Pugh come immediately to mind. The same story holds true of women too, in general, although they have been more inclined to have two champion singles players pair together to make an unbeatable doubles combination. Louise Brough and Margaret Osborne, Shirley Fry and Doris Hart, and Pam Shriver and Martina Navratilova are examples of that. But once you get past such duos, you find the same sort of specialist doubles geniuses among the women as the men. Elizabeth Ryan is a particularly good example, and Wendy Turnbull is another. Sarah Palfrey Danzig, great singles player that she certainly was, seemed to perform even more brilliantly on the doubles court, and with a variety of partners.

But who would even think of the Frenchwoman, Françoise Durr, when trying to recall especially wonderful doubles specialists? Despite owning the strangest and apparently not very effective service ever seen in major championship tennis, Durr won the French doubles championship five times in a row, 1967–1971, with two different partners. One was a very fine player, the British Ann Haydon Jones, but the other was a considerably less highly ranked performer, Gail Sheriff Chanfreau, and it made no difference with whom Durr was partnered—she won. Durr herself was no great shakes as a singles player, but in doubles she, and one or the other of her partners, beat such outstanding

97

teams as Billie Jean King and Rosie Casals, and Margaret Smith Court and Nancy Richey. One could hardly do better than that, but Durr reached the finals of the women's doubles at Wimbledon five times, partnering with four different women, and won the U.S. championship twice, with Darlene Hard in 1969 and with Betty Stove in 1972, and was a runner-up in the U.S. event on two other occasions as well. It is strikingly clear that Françoise Durr had to be somebody that anyone would be lucky to draw as a doubles partner, even if there were a number of better singles players available.

Getting back to you and the here and now, what has all this history got to do with your chances of playing quality tennis when you reach an age that's considered advanced in sports? I would hope a great deal, because it's inspiring for a quite ordinary singles player to learn that when he makes the inevitable decision to concentrate on the tactical game of doubles, he has a chance to become the indispensable member of a team that may achieve a lot more respect than he ever did as a singles contestant. In doubles, "savvy" counts for just about as much as fluent strokes or a punishing overhead. A player who is not endowed with the outstanding talent that's required to become a star individual player can, by being able to exploit the many nuances of doubles strategy, become the vital cog in a doubles combination. Obviously, if you are an over-50 player, your goals are set not on laurels in one of the Grand Slam tournaments but on the fun and pride you can get by competing well in your age bracket for the doubles title in a local area. The last chapter of this book will tell you how and where to find opportunities to enter such tournaments, or create them in your own community.

The first consideration in embarking on a doubles match, or a doubles tournament, or a doubles career (some seniors who have retired actually do this, following the sun wherever it shines best throughout the year), is to look for a compatible partner. If you have the soul of a pot-hunter, and we all do have at least a trace of it, and would rather win a plated trophy in a tennis tournament than experience any other joy in life, you'll start out by looking for the best player you can find who might be willing to be your partner. That may turn out to be a profitable quest, and you may go on to glory and a plated trophy, but don't be too sure. If there isn't a really substantial difference between the talents of two potential partners, choose the one with whom you have a solid rapport, even if he's only rated a 3.5 player and the other man is a 4.0. This makes sense from two standpoints. First, a doubles team that works in concert has a great edge over a pair who are at odds with each other frequently and who, even when they don't criticize each other's play or strategy (and many do), smolder with resentment and self-pity. Such a team can be beaten, even if they are better players than you and your partner. And second, remember that enjoying a game is the prime reason for going out and playing in the first place. You can have more fun losing with a partner you like— where you have each learned to mesh your respective games—than winning with a partner who annoys you—and where teamwork has been subordinated to individualism.

Of course, most senior tennis players aren't married to just one doubles partner, unless they are trying to forge a combination with serious intent to play in tournaments. Most of us are part of a regular group of tennis-playing friends or acquaintances, and new partnerships are formed each time people play, and often changed after each set. One of the pleasantest tennis sessions that can be planned for a number of people is a well-run round robin tournament, where partnerships change regularly after a certain number of games, usually four. The attempt is to have everybody play with everybody else, or as close to it as time and the number of courts available will allow. The last chapter will offer some suggestions about getting information and running a round robin in your community. As a round robin player, you obviously can't work up much rapport with a partner whom you have only for a few games before another one comes along, so the wisest and most pleasant thing to do is just to play along with each, never criticizing, and tossing out a smile or a pat on the back whenever one is deserved. You can't reform a partner whom you'll have only for a few games, and even if he needs reforming, it should come from someone other than his tennis partner. Besides, being a good guy with a number of partners is good training to be a good guy when you hook up with a partner with whom you hope to play regularly, in a tournament or even throughout a season.

Let's say you've found one. You're both happy about your forthcoming partnership, and now you've got to get your heads together and decide a few things:

1. Is one of you a better server, and the other a better net player? If so, in each set be sure you start out with that setup in your first service game. If you do, you'll usually have one extra game per set with your strengths where they perform best, rather than one less game. And since a team does not have to follow the order of service after a set is concluded, and can start afresh in the following set, it makes sense to grasp that advantage each time you can.

If neither of you is clearly the superior server or net player, or if one of you is clearly better at both, you'll just have to discuss matters and decide which setup is likely to work best for you when your team is serving. If you know anything about your opponents' strengths or weaknesses, that might be the factor on which you base your decision. Against strong opposition that returns serves extremely well, you'd probably choose to have your strong server start things off for you, and take your chances on what the net man may or may not be able to do. Against a weaker team that doesn't attack at all when receiving service, you might do better to have your less severe server begin, and have the better volleyer up at net, poised to cut off and put away any weak returns.

2. If you win the spin of the racquet, should you automatically choose to serve first, as most singles players and doubles teams do? If you are both good enough servers to feel pretty confident that you'll be winning very nearly all games when you're serving, then by all means choose to serve first so that, if form holds, you'll have the edge of being ahead one game on the odd game throughout the set, and your opponents will always be in the position of having to play catch-up. But if your serves are not that reliable, *or if your opponents' serves are not*, there are some good reasons to choose to receive first. One was discussed earlier—when an opponent's serve is extremely weak, a factor frequently found among senior players who do little more than waft the ball into play. A return off a weak serve can often be a more aggressive shot than one's own serve, and can put your team on the attack. Another possible advantage in choosing to receive first is that it gives your team a chance to settle down in a game it's supposed to lose anyway, while the other team is pressured to win that first service game, because it's supposed to do so. That often causes them to commit unforced errors at the outset, before they get their sea legs, so to speak, and lose the game. Then if your team, warmed up by now, manages to hold serve, you are off to a 2-0 lead, and have the break needed to win a set. A third reason why you might not choose to serve first is that there are circumstances, such as sun and wind conditions, where choosing which end of the court you'd prefer to begin on can be more of an advantage than serving first. (If that's your thinking, and you win the racquet spin, make it clear you're choosing which end you want to start on, and don't carelessly say merely that you want to receive first, as you would do in the other cases above. Unless you specify that, an alert opponent will not only be serving first, but will be able to choose the end from which he'll be doing it.)

3. When your team is receiving, which of you is going to play in the deuce court and which in the ad court? On the whole, the usual answer to this is that the cagier and steadier of the two of you, the one with better command of the more subtle shots such as the dink and the lob, is more valuable in the deuce court, while the big hitter and more severe volleyer and overhead smasher—probably the better singles player—is best situated in the ad court. But this is only a general rule of thumb, to which there can be many exceptions in normal club play. Let it be noted, however, that in international play, the doubles geniuses mentioned previously were almost invariably deuce court specialists.

One of you may be left-handed, and thus probably better placed in the ad court. That is the conventional alignment most right-handed/left-handed combinations favor, figuring that both will be receiving serves for the most part on their respective forehands. One school of thought reverses things, putting the left-hander on the right side and the right-hander on the left, its theory being that it is better to concentrate the forehand strength of a team down the middle. A few exceptionally strong righty-southpaw teams in the past have played this way and won, but most pairs, even of world class, adopt the orthodox positioning, which is certainly the more sensible alignment for doubles teams of more modest talent. It's a decided advantage for both players to be able to return most serves off their forehands, while choosing the other alignment puts pressure on both players' backhands; furthermore, it isn't always a good idea to have both forehands ready for shots up the middle—sometimes it causes confusion about which partner should take a shot, and anything from a clash of racquets to a nasty injury can occur when two eager partners go all-out for the same ball.

If you are both southpaws, you will probably (but not necessarily) want to reverse the first general rule, and station the solider player on the left and the smasher on the right. Here the best reason to do so is to allow the more severe smasher to take most of any lobs that come his team's way on his forehand.

4. How aggressive are the two of you going to be? You've got several choices, but only one of them is going to make your doubles team a really strong one. On the other hand, success may not be your immediate goal, and all you're aiming for is to play your respectable brand of quality tennis, and have fun. In that case, choosing one of the other options can make sense, particularly if not working yourself too hard is a physical concern for you. Look over the various options open to you and your partner, considering their merits and their faults, and you may be able to lay the groundwork to approaching the best game, in all senses, that the two of you can pull off.

Option A. This is the way every really good doubles team wants to play, and it's the way you should try to play until and unless the time comes when you decide you just can't. I hope that time never comes but if it does, there are other optional ways of playing, which will be analyzed later, that can be just as much fun, and they can be winning ways too. This first option is the best because if the talents of two competing doubles teams are equal, the team playing the way Option A says doubles should be played is virtually certain to beat the equally talented players who are not playing that way.

This strategy involves both players making every effort to get upcourt near the net, side by side, at the very earliest opportunity. When your team is serving, that would be right away, after the serve. The server follows his delivery in, probably making a volley at midcourt en route, unless his partner, already at net, has managed to intercept the return. He then continues forward to join his partner at the net with another step or two. That's the ideal way for a doubles team to achieve that commanding position, but it doesn't come easily for the server. He's not only got to hustle all the way, but he's got to be able to make a strong, forcing volley from midcourt or the whole thing is likely to boomerang against his team. This can be tiring stuff for an over-50 player, but then it only occurs once every four games in doubles, which isn't too bad. If, as an older player, you find you simply cannot do this, an alternative is to take the return on the bounce, drive the ball back and *then* follow it in to join your partner at net. This is a lot easier on the server and, since the principle of getting a team side by side up at the net as soon as possible is being observed as

105

much as possible, it qualifies as being an acceptable variation of Option A.

If the server commits a fault on his first serve, and has to fall back on a safe, weaker second serve, he's likely to stay back anyway, and wait before coming up, in the same fashion as above. Both players at net as often as possible is easier to accomplish when your team is serving, of course, but don't overlook the possibility that under certain circumstances it can be done when your team is receiving. Those circumstances occur most often when one of you is consistently able to return a modestly paced serve with a strong, cross-court drive back to the server who, having missed his first serve, is not scuttling up to midcourt, but is staying back fairly near the baseline. The other of you on the receiving team, standing in his normal position at the rear of the service box while the first serve is attempted, knows that his partner is going to pounce on the second serve and follow it in, just as if he were serving rather than receiving. So he, as he sees the second "safe" serve being delivered, skips up to the net himself, instead of holding his position, and is joined there a moment later by his partner. Now the receiving team is at net and on the attack, and the only thing that is likely to dislodge them is a perfect lob. Any doubles team worth its salt will take a chance on being able to handle that, in exchange for the opportunity to form a pretty impregnable wall at net. There's an additional advantage in the receiver's partner going all the way to the net on that second serve. If he were to hold his position at the rear of the service box, and the opponent were to hit a good, low, topspin return, he'd be apt to be caught in no man's land and have to make a weak half volley at best, whereas if he's up at net he's in position to put away a winning volley.

Since in good doubles, the serving team is always striving to get to the net, and the receiving team is sometimes trying to do so too, both can succeed on the same point now and then. The sight (if you're a spectator) or the excitement (if you're one of the players) of two doubles teams, both near the net and slugging or jockeying it out eyeball to eyeball, is one of the most exhilarating delights of doubles: it has no real counterpart in the game of singles.

Of course, as indicated earlier, these tactics may be asking too much of many older players. Apart from the desirability of storming the net as much as possible, there's the problem of scampering back from it to try to handle a lob hit over one's head. Since each player is responsible for his half of the court when a team is attempting to play in this style, there's no calling of "Yours, partner!" when a good lob is tossed up over your head. It's up to you to get back and try to angle or smash it back, or at least to keep the ball in play. This can be a pretty daunting task for any but a well-conditioned athlete, and when you read here that it's up to you, you may well react with "Who, *me*?" Fair enough if that's the case, and we'll go into your other options next, but if you're aiming for the best and you're physically able to do it, you must shoot to set up that barrier at the net side by side with your partner, and then wreak havoc upon your opponents from that position.

Option B. The tactic of having one player up near the net and the other back near the baseline is recognized as the basic and best strategy for winning doubles.

What's wrong with that sentence?

What's wrong is that, unfortunately, it refers to the game of badminton. It certainly is not true of tennis. All top-level teams shun letting themselves get into the "one up, one back" position, but most club-level players are likely to play that way most of the time. Usually the reason is not failure to recognize that the system has its weaknesses when up against parallel net-rushers. Rather it's because it demands less of a player physically, and he can keep going a long time more if he doesn't have the obligation to get up to the net all the time, and then to continue to cover his half of the court when forced back from the net by a lob. If the server stays back, and the receiver hits a lob over the net man's head, there's not even any need for the net man to call "Yours, partner!" The server will be darting over to take the shot the second he sees what it is as a matter of course, and his partner, at net, will slide over to the other side of the court. This works out splendidly in badminton, and it works out well enough in tennis too—up to a point. That point is reached if you and your friends play that way, but you then run up against a team whose strokes may be no better than yours and your partner's, but who work in concert to dominate the net against you.

108

But be of moderately good cheer anyhow. In senior doubles of less than super-seniors caliber, you'll encounter many more teams that play your way and so have no advantage, than you will teams that play like Ken Flach and Robert Seguso. This is particularly true of mixed doubles, where the physical prospect of having to play so energetic a game inhibits many players from even trying to do so. If you are one such, don't be ashamed of belonging to the club. Most senior tennis players, certainly most over 60, are members of it too, and they enjoy playing, and win their share of matches. For although they have a handicap when facing a "both up" team of comparable quality, many a "one up, one back" team has been able to overcome that handicap by playing quality tennis, while their opponents didn't.

Option C. There is another option, which is not too often seen among eager tennis players, but which can work out very well on occasion and which certainly is easiest on the human frame. That is the tactic of both players staying back near the baseline most but not necessarily all of the time. The server's partner does not take up a position at net: he stands near or a little in front of the baseline on the side of the court away from his serving partner. When the team is receiving, the person not being served to does not position himself up near midcourt or forecourt: he stays back as well. Essentially baseliners who enjoy scrambling after angled shots that seem out of their reach, and are good at it, a team like this gives the impression that they never heard of volleying or net play. But two circumstances arise frequently—and a good team of this sort has to be up to each occasion. When one member has made a particularly effective forcing drive or a devastatingly accurate deep lob, and the circumstances indicate that any return is apt to be a feeble one, a backcourt duo worthy of its salt will seize such an opportunity and rush up to the net together, ready to punish such a return. The other occasion is when an opposing player tries a drop shot, which obviously draws up at least one of the baseline lurkers. If it's a good drop shot, it may win the point from our team outright: if it's a poor drop shot it probably will boomerang, which is enough to discourage too many drop shots being attempted. So most of the time our baseline duo can indeed stay back, the disadvantage being that when they run up against a pair of adept netrushers, the odds are going to be against them.

A team that plays this way probably is composed of two very steady, reliable strokers of the ball, with both of them being superior defensive players, able to stand up against and block back smashes, and willing to scramble all day to whatever far reaches the situation demands. They are basically singles players who, perhaps somewhat uneasily, find themselves playing doubles. Sometimes such a team's members understand each other so well, and complement each other so effectively, that they can beat another team that appears to be much stronger. An outstanding example was the team of brothers, Howard and Bob Kinsey, who won the doubles championship of the United States in 1924, lobbing to death the flashiest, best doubles teams in the world—unbeatable, until they ran up against the Kinseys.

It is worth noting that, even if you don't think much of your doubles team playing this way as a regular thing, it can work out well to adopt it now and then. If, for example, you are normally a "one up, one back" duo, but the opponents are giving the server a constant headache by popping the ball back so artfully over the head of the server's partner at net that the server has the toughest time trying to cover the shots, the "both back" position might be an effective answer—at least for a while. Later, when your opponents lose their miraculous touch on lobs—and these things do come and go as a rule—you can revert to your normal style of play, if you still wish to do so. In any case, apart from trying to counter a situation, as in the above, often doing something different—*anything* different —can unsettle opponents who are giving you fits, and spark you with fresh impetus. Bill Tilden, the master strategist of them all, dictated the ten most famous words in tennis instruction: "Never change a winning game. Always change a losing game."

Modern major tournament doubles suffers because the financial rewards are so much greater for singles that many stars don't compete in doubles at all. Others, who do, simply hit out as if they were playing singles, not having given much time or thought or practice to doubles. With them doubles is a sideline pastime of not much importance while singles is their living. There are modern exceptions, of course, great singles players like John McEnroe and Martina Navratilova who love

111

and understand doubles as well and have won a flock of doubles championships, but they are the exceptions. Generally speaking, the winner of one of the Grand Slam singles tournaments, particularly in the men's division, is not even entered in the doubles.

That may make sense for such players, whose interest in tennis is heavily conditioned by what it means to their bankroll, but you are in a different situation. As a senior player, doubles is the game you'll be playing for the most part and I'd bet you're going to be glad of it. There's so much more variety to good doubles that the game can be much more fun than singles, and fun is synonymous with your primary aim—the enjoyment of playing tennis. So let's assume that you are going to concentrate on doubles, and playing doubles as well as you possibly can. A good first step is to consider what made some of those winning old-time specialists so good at doubles. For one thing, games didn't depend so completely on powerful serving, and the holding of all the service games, as they do now. Players were prepared to defend all the way, and points were not conceded lightly. Attack was combined with staunch defense, and doubles was a game of infinite finesse. The great doubles teams, like George Lott and John Van Ryn, or Van Ryn and Wilmer Allison, or Billy Talbert and Gardnar Mulloy, attacked whenever they saw the chance, and defended just as ardently when they got into trouble. Points went on for a while; these days it's pretty much all attack, and points are concluded much more quickly. It's not as much fun either for spectator or contestant, and fun

112

is what we older tennis players are looking for. The idea of being on the attack constantly, and getting up to the net side by side, is clearly the way the very best doubles teams win. If you can do it, blessings on you and your partner, but most of us are not numbered among the very best doubles teams and simply must do what we can to win. At our level, the real trick in playing quality doubles is to keep our opponents guessing. Simply slugging the ball is not as effective as it often can be in singles, for with only half a court for each person to cover, sheer speed doesn't overwhelm opponents often. But varied positioning, varied spin, and other surprises can carry the day a lot of the time.

What is meant by varied positioning? An obvious variation would be one's position when serving, which can range anywhere from the extreme corner almost to the midcourt mark on the baseline. Most unthinking doubles players invariably continue to serve from exactly the same spot as they did previously, whether doing so from the right court or the left. Since they're usually facing right-handed opponents, they're likely to take a position fairly close to the midpoint when serving from the right, but farther out toward the corner when serving from the left, figuring that those positions make it easier in each case to serve to an opponent's backhand. So they do it every time. Well, the reasoning is fair enough, but it's not an eternal truth. For one thing, it isn't really so very much easier to serve to a particular place from one particular place: if you have decent control of direction, you can aim the ball where you want to from any position on the baseline. For another, everyone encounters plenty of left-handers these days, and when you do, sticking blindly to routine produces exactly the wrong effect. But finally, and most important, opponents can get into a groove about meeting and successfully returning your serve, if it always comes over the net in the same way, from the same starting place. If you vary your serving position from time to time, so that the ball moves toward the receiver on a different diagonal line, it can bother him considerably.

If your partner is serving, and you are at net, you can often give the receiver something confusing to think about by occasionally varying your regular position. Move over a step farther than usual toward midcourt. He'll suspect you'll be trying to poach on his return, and one result may be that he'll angle his return too sharply, to keep it away from you, and hit the ball out over the sideline. Or he may decide to try to shoot a passing drive down your now somewhat exposed alley. This attempt is known as "keeping the net man honest," meaning that if you think he is capable of making the shot, you will from then on be quite reluctant ever to try poaching. However, in this case he's in for a surprise, because you never had any intention of poaching on that point. You were merely trying to fake him by false-positioning yourself and leaning toward midcourt as your partner hit his serve, but what you actually did was to move back immediately thereafter to cover the possibility that the receiver might try to pass you down the alley. And what do you know? Here the ball comes, right at you, and *wham!* Your point, and an opponent who from now on will have one more complication to think about when he's receiving, and you're at net.

One variation that a doubles team can assume on occasion is the epitome of the unusual. In the United States it is known as the Australian formation; in Australia they refer to it as the American formation. This is because, in Davis Cup competition, quite independently and a number of years apart, first one nation used it to help defeat a doubles team from the other nation, and later the other nation retaliated, using the same ploy. Today, both nations usually call it the tandem formation, which may go to show that international diplomacy sometimes emerges triumphant.

In any case, in the tandem formation the partner of the server stands at the net, but not in his usual position of facing the receiver. Instead he stands on the same half of the court as the server. This opens up one side of the court completely, of course, but only temporarily, because the moment the serve is struck, the server scurries over into the undefended court to handle the return if it's directed there, as it very likely will be. What may equally well happen, however, is that the receiver, accustomed to hitting a cross-court return to keep the ball away from the net man, now sees the net man standing just where he regularly aims his return. He's understandably upset about not being sure just what he should do under these circumstances, and whatever he does may turn out to be catastrophic. What he actually does a surprisingly high percentage of the time is the most catastrophic of all. He makes an unforced error, and his team loses the point immediately.

The tandem formation does have its weaknesses, of course, or it would be used much more than it is. A perfectly hit return into the alley of the exposed half court will be a tough shot for the server to dash over to and handle well, if he can do it at all. And a deep, topspin lob over the net man's head to the far corner is almost a sure winner for the receiver if he's able to execute that shot. So the tandem is not a strategy to be used all the time, but it's a first-rate one to throw into the pot now and then.

Actually I have one old doubles friend, Sam, who liked to play the tandem formation, along with his partner, every time he served from the left-hand court. Sam is right-handed and had an excellent forehand, but a comparatively weak backhand—more of a poke than a stroke. So if he was serving from the left with his partner in the customary net position on the right, Sam had his problems if the receiver did the comparatively simple thing of returning Sam's serve cross-court to Sam's backhand. But look what happened with the tandem formation! Sam served and instantly scampered over to his right, getting there in plenty of time to meet a return hit into that court with his strong forehand. But if the receiver tried a cross-court return, it had to be a perfect one, or Sam's partner would be in position to put it away. (This story about Sam is an unusual case of the possible virtues of trying the tandem. I have written it in the past tense because it happened years ago. However, I am happy to report that Sam is still playing, and no longer feels the necessity of calling upon the tandem whenever he serves from the ad court, for Sam has learned how to hit a backhand!)

Varying your position when receiving service is pretty much a matter of paying attention to the server's position, and the type of serve he employs on his first ball and on his second. Obviously, if he's a person who varies his position from serve to serve, you'll shift one way or the other too, to try to counter any advantage he's trying to obtain. If he puts a lot of spin on his serve, you'll find out in what direction the bounce will take the ball, and will take your receiving position to allow for it. This often means that, apart from probably moving forward as a second serve is being directed toward you, you may be varying your position sideways, to allow for the excessive spin usually imparted on second serves.

Incidentally, as far as moving up is concerned, there is a ploy you can sometimes try, after your opponent has committed a fault on his first serve. Move up quite far—well past where you'd be comfortable about returning his serve if he got it in—as he's about to serve his second ball, *and make sure he sees you do it!* Actually, this is quite like the fake poaching motion of the net man, who then actually retreated to cover his alley, which I mentioned a few paragraphs ago. Here you too are faking, and you skip back a few feet into your more accustomed receiving position as the server makes his toss into the air, when he surely won't be watching you anymore. Afraid that you're still really

117

far forward into court and ready to pounce on any weak serve, he tries to put extra punch into his second serve. With what result? Surprisingly often, a double fault.

Now please believe me. I wrote the above paragraph early in the spring of 1989, when I was working on the first draft of this book. It was a tactic I had used every now and then for years to good effect, and I thought it was my own private little ploy. But in July 1989, a good three months later, the tactic was used at a most critical moment in a most thrilling match in the French Open. Although Michael Chang amazed the tennis world by going on to win this major Grand Slam event, the biggest match the 17-year-old had was his quarter-final affair against the tournament's overwhelming favorite, the number-one player in the world, Ivan Lendl. Chang lost the first two sets to Lendl, but then, sticking to his guns with incredible fortitude, he won the next two sets and got to match point in the fifth set, with Lendl serving. Lendl's first serve was a fault, and that's the moment when Chang boldly moved up to take his receiving position no more than a couple of feet behind the service box. The difference between what Chang did and the gambit I propose is that Chang wasn't faking—he intended to hold his ground and, if Lendl put the ball into court, meet it quickly with what at best would have been a sort of half volley. But that is not the point. Just seeing Chang dare him to deliver an effective second serve intimidated the world's top ranking player into catching the tape on the top of the net on a serve that was hit with enough punch that the ball then soared up and well past the service box for a double fault! Game, set, and match to Michael Chang!

Now this is a perfectly legitimate way of using a little psychology to try to unnerve an opponent. There are a number that are not, such as "quick serving" an opponent. True, if somebody tries that on you, you can circumvent it merely by refusing to play the serve, claiming you were not ready, but often you don't react quickly enough, and do attempt to return a serve that really has caught you unawares, so then you lose the point. "Quick serving" purposely is despicable; faking one's position is not.

At this point, and in this connection, for no reason except to give you pleasure, I cannot resist offering a few pages from a certain book to any reader who has never experienced the joy of reading it. This classic, published about forty years ago and now long out of print, is *Gamesmanship, or the Art of Winning at Games Without Actually Cheating*, by Stephen Potter, a British humorist. The term he coined, "gamesmanship," achieved such recognition that it became part of the language, and you can find it in your dictionary. Anyhow, one of the funniest sections in Potter's book concerns tennis, and here it is, along with its accompanying illustration:

> *8th June 1931.*
> But it was in that changing-room after a certain game of lawn tennis in 1931 that the curtain was lifted, and I began to see. In those days I used to play lawn tennis for a small but progressive London College—Birkbeck, where

I lectured. It happened that my partner at that time was C. Joad, the celebrated gamesman, who in his own sphere is known as metaphysician and educationist. Our opponents were usually young men from the larger colleges, competing against us not only with the advantage of age but also with a decisive advantage in style. They would throw the service ball very high in the modern manner: the back-hands, instead of being played from the navel, were played, in fact, on the back-hand, weight on right foot, in the exaggerated copy-book style of the time—a method of play which tends to reduce all games, as I believe, to a barrack-square drill by numbers; but, nevertheless, of acknowledged effectiveness.

In one match we found ourselves opposite a couple of particularly tall and athletic young men of this type from University College. We will call them Smith and Brown. The knock-up showed that, so far as play was concerned, Joad and I, playing for Birkbeck, had no chance. U. C. won the toss. It was Smith's service, and he cracked down a cannon-ball to Joad which moved so fast that Joad, while making some effort to suggest by his attitude that he had thought the ball was going to be a fault, nevertheless was unable to get near with his racket, which he did not even attempt to move. Score: fifteen-love. Service to me. I had had time to gauge the speed of this serve, and the next one did, in fact, graze the edge of my racket-frame. Thirty-love. Now Smith was serving again to

Joad—who this time, as the ball came straight towards him, was able, by grasping the racket firmly with both hands, to receive the ball on the strings, whereupon the ball shot back to the other side and volleyed into the stop-netting near the ground behind Brown's feet.

Now here comes the moment on which not only this match, but so much of the future of British sport was to turn. Score: forty-love. Smith at S^1 (see Fig. 1) is about to cross over to serve to me (at P). When Smith gets to a point (K) *not less than one foot and not more than two feet* beyond the centre of the court (I know now what I only felt then—that timing is everything in this gambit), Joad (standing at J^2) called across the net, in an even tone:

"Kindly say clearly, please, whether the ball was in or out."

Crude to our ears, perhaps. A Stone-Age implement. But beautifully accurate gamesmanship for 1931. For the student must realise that these two young men were both in the highest degree charming, well-mannered young men, perfect in their sportsmanship and behavior. Smith (at point K) stopped dead.

> SMITH: I'm so sorry—I *thought* it was out. (*The ball had hit the back netting twelve feet behind him before touching the ground.*) But what did you think, Brown?
>
> BROWN: I *thought* it was out—but do let's have it again.

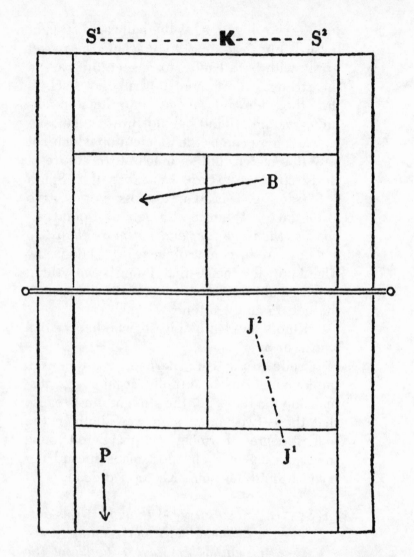

FIG. 1. *Key:* P = Potter, J = Joad, S = Smith, B = Brown. The dotted line represents Smith's path from S¹ to S². K represents the point he has reached on the cross-over when Joad has moved along the line (dot and dash) J¹ (where he had tried to return Smith's service) to J². Smith having arrived at, but not further than, the point K on the line S¹–S², J (Joad) speaks.

JOAD: No, I don't want to have it again. I only want you to say clearly, if you will, whether the ball is in or out.

There is nothing more putting off to young university players than a slight suggestion that their etiquette or sportsmanship is in question. How well we know this fact, yet how often we forget to make use of it. Smith sent a double fault to me, and another double fault to Joad. He did not get in another ace service till halfway through the third set of a match which incidentally we won.

That night I thought hard and long. Could not this simple gambit of Joad's be extended to include other aspects of the game—to include all games? For me, it was the birth of gamesmanship.

To get back to serious business, many of us, as we get a little older—and slower—on a tennis court, are told by our doctors or our mates to give up singles, and play doubles exclusively. On the whole, as you know by now, I consider this good advice. But before turning the final page on the discussion, I'd like to extol the virtues of a certain stepchild of the game of tennis that seems to me particularly geared for older players, who may grudgingly concede that they should give up playing singles, but are unwilling to do so— at least not completely.

This form of the game has no officially recognized name, and it isn't even mentioned in the Rules of

Tennis. It's also usually played only as a sort of disappointing consolation when one player in a scheduled doubles match fails to show up, and three players are left cursing him. What they then do is play what most of us informally call "Canadian doubles," for no known reason. Casual investigation has failed to reveal if Canadians play it at all or, if they do, if they call it that.

No matter. It happens to be a splendid game, offering attractive features that in some ways more than compensate for the cancellation of the scheduled doubles match. Let's say the three players who are left and who have decided to play Canadian doubles are Green, Black, and White. By lot one of them, let's say Green, will start playing alone in one court against the doubles team of Black and White. Green can hit into their entire doubles court, but they have to confine their shots to his singles court. In essence, he's playing singles against their playing doubles, with somewhat compensating advantages on both sides. He has a wider court to attack than he would normally have if playing singles, but he's up against two players. The doubles pair have that advantage but, of course, the disadvantage of having to confine their shots to the narrower boundaries of a singles court. The doubles team should have the edge and should win usually, but by no means always.

They play this way for three games, with Green serving the middle game between the games served by the other two. After that, one of the other two—let's say Black—takes over as the singles player, and Green joins White to compete as a doubles team against him. Three more games are now played, with Black serving the middle one, and then it's White's turn to play alone in the singles court and compete against the other two, for three more games.

The triumvirate will now have played a total of nine games—more or less the equivalent of one set. The score for each will be very low, however, for the only games that count are the ones won by the singles player, so the maximum score any one of them can attain is three games—more often it will be two, or one, or none. Not to worry. They've only played something like one set, and surely are ready to start another round of nine games, and very probably a third. How long does this go on? As long as their inclination lasts, and as long as the entire informality of this makeshift game makes sense.

The players may decide to play until some one of them wins six games. They may decide to play the twenty-seven games involved in three full rotations and then quit, with the winner being the person who has won more games than the others. Or they may simply play until their scheduled time on court has run out, and not worry about whether some one or two of them didn't get "last licks." It's that sort of game, and its very casualness can provide unusual fun on a tennis court, to say nothing of the variety in play that each changing situation requires.

More significantly, for what this book is aimed at, Canadian doubles is a game that over-50 players might actually prefer playing to the other more conventional forms of tennis. They might well plan to play it from the outset, rather than simply be forced to fall back on it, when the fourth member of a doubles match disappoints.

Why? Well, playing a game that for one third of the time offers a player a challenge comparable to that of the singles game, but then allows him more or less to coast physically for two thirds of the time while being partnered in a doubles team, is a marvelous compromise solution for the veteran who knows he should give up high-pressure singles competition, but doesn't want to forsake singles entirely. It's a regimen of which even his doctor or his mate could well approve.

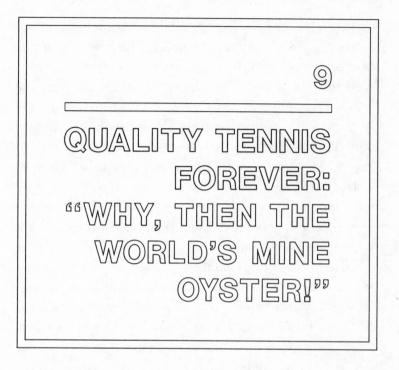

9

QUALITY TENNIS FOREVER: "WHY, THEN THE WORLD'S MINE OYSTER!"

As people grow older, in many ways they can begin to feel out of things. Certainly, that's likely to be true of anyone who retires from an active office life. It's also often the case socially, as new and younger people emerge and seem to become the important ones in gatherings that you used to frequent, and where you were recognized as one belonging to the inner circle.

Be of good cheer. An older tennis player never has to join a Lonely Hearts Club. He may continue to play with old friends, or his children and their friends, but even if he's neither lucky enough nor good enough to continue to enjoy close bonds like these, there are many tens of thousands of veteran tennis players all across the country who play tennis and delight in it well into their 80s. They value the game as a way not only of keeping fit, but as a way of enhancing the quality of life, both recreationally and socially. All new-comers who share those feelings are welcome to their camp. You can become one of their number even if, until now, you've been more or less of a hermit and, far from being instinctively gregarious, have always been shy about meeting new people. A love of tennis makes the world kin.

If you want to expand your horizons, and have no idea how to go about it, a splendid first step you can take is to send $6.50 to the United States Tennis Association Publications Department, 707 Alexander Road, Princeton, NJ 08540, and ask to be sent a copy of the *USTA Senior Tennis Directory*. (The price is $5.00; the extra $1.50 is for shipping and handling.) Apart from the fact that there is a lot of other interesting material in it, from USTA services of many sorts and three informative articles about why seniors play tennis (Social Aspect by Ronald B. Woods, Ph.D.; Psychological Aspect by James E, Loehr, Ed.D.; Sport Science Aspect by Irving V. Glick, M.D.), the booklet would be well worth the money if it contained only the nationwide directory that it does. Information about what clubs and facilities exist in each city that offers programs for over-50 players is given, state by state, with each program described and whom to contact if you're interested in joining, or in getting more information. Simply to give you an idea, here are eight sample entries, taken at random out of the more than 225 listed in the most current (1988) directory, reprinted with the permission of the United States Tennis Association:

ARIZONA, City of Phoenix. The Parks Recreation and Library Department holds group tennis lessons and tournaments for over 200 seniors in the 50, 60, and 70-and-over age categories. Senior participants, 220. Contact Larry P. Piper, 1802 N. West Encato Boulevard, Phoenix, AZ 85007. (602) 262-6481.

CALIFORNIA, Corona Del Mar. City of Newport Beach. The Oasis Tennis team provides informal play and social activity in the afternoon for intermediate-level seniors. Classes in the morning for seniors at all levels. Senior participants: 100. Contact Celeste Jareine-Haug, City of Newport Beach, City Hall–Oasis Senior Center, 800 Marguerite Avenue, Corona del Mar, CA 92625. (714) 644-3245.

FLORIDA, City of Clearwater. Many senior activities are planned at the McMullen Tennis Complex including challenge ladders, round robins, team matches, tournaments and Olympics. Senior participants: 200. Contact Tom Walbolt, McMullen Tennis Complex, 1000 Edenville Avenue, Clearwater, FL 34624. (813) 462-6144.

INDIANA, Indianapolis Racquet Club East. The Silver Foxes for men over 55 and the Foxy Ladies for senior ladies meet three days per week for two hours of mixer tennis and instruction. Senior participants: 100. Contact Clair Hilliker, 4901 Shadeland Avenue, Indianapolis, IN 46226. (317) 545-2228.

MICHIGAN, Grand Rapids. East Hills Athletic Club. East Hills has approximately 500 senior tennis members who arrange their own games on a permanent court-time basis. Contact Tom Essenburg, East Hills Athletic Club, 1640 East Paris, Grand Rapids, MI 49546. (616) 942-9521.

MINNESOTA, St. Louis Park. Senior Tennis Players Club, Inc. The organization schedules tennis play, usually doubles, for its 1200 members on reserved outdoor courts in summer and indoor facilities in winter, at 8 to 10 locations. For a small fee, members receive the list of places and times for play, the captains' names for reservations, and the monthly newsletter. Free beginners' lessons are available. Contact Mandy Johnson, Senior Tennis Players Club, Inc., 5200 West 28th Street, St. Louis Park, MN 55416. (612) 922-4327.

NEW YORK, Rochester. Mid-Town Tennis Club. Tennis Five-O is designed to introduce or reacquaint adults over 50 to tennis. Senior participants: 302. Contact Nancy Welch, Mid-Town Tennis Club, 55 Gould Street, Rochester, NY 14610. (716) 461-2300.

WASHINGTON, Bellevue. P.R.O. Club. Over 300 seniors play tennis regularly at this large health club in such events as "the Century

Tournament," the 45+ Tournament, and Play-Instruct sessions. They also take part in Mixed Madness, Pro-Am doubles, get-acquainted nights, and a computerized ladder. Contact Paul Moseby, P.R.O. Club, 4455 148th Avenue N.E., Bellevue, WA 98007. (206) 885-5566.

What's the matter? Do you live in Massachusetts or North Carolina or Oregon, and you feel left out? Are you attracted by what the Senior Tennis Players Club in St. Louis Park has to offer, but you've no intention of moving to Minnesota? Well, I couldn't give you more than that tiniest taste of the more than a couple of hundred other tennis locations that are in the *USTA Senior Tennis Directory* without impinging unduly on that publication's territory, so you'd better send for the directory itself. I myself didn't know about it at the time, a little over a year ago, when my wife and I spent a couple of weeks housesitting for our daughter and son-in-law, who live in Princeton, New Jersey, but who were off on a trip. If I had been aware of the directory and had a copy of it, I'd have found out that by phoning Craig H. Smith, who lives at 627 Kingston Road, Princeton, NJ 08540, and whose number is (609) 924-4256, I could join the Princeton Seniors during my stay. That's a group that meets three times a week throughout the year, usually at the "early bird hours" (7:30-9:30 A.M).

The fact is that my daughter, Kathy, knowing that we were coming to housesit for her, and that I'd have to be wheeled off to the loony bin if I couldn't get in any tennis for two weeks, did some investigating, and found Craig Smith by herself. After talking to her, he laid out the welcome mat for me and, as a result, I was able to enjoy half a dozen sessions of the highest quality doubles any visiting senior could desire. There are more than eighty players in the 50+, 60+, 70+ range who are signed up with this group, and the indefatigable Mr. Smith invariably corrals at least two to three dozen of them to play doubles each time out. He arranges the pairings astutely, since he knows the levels at which the old-timers play and he soon familiarizes himself with the quality of any visitor, like myself. He gets to the courts before 7:30 and posts a schedule for the matches he has arranged for that day, and invariably they result in spirited, jovial encounters.

I admired some of the players enough to try to get some perspectives other than my own that I could incorporate into this book. So before leaving, I distributed a letter to the members of the group, telling about the forthcoming book, and saying that I'd welcome receiving any letters recounting experiences, or advice, or stratagems that were unusual enough not to be familiar to most older players, including me. I did get half a dozen letters—one quite touching about how that player's late-in-life love affair with tennis had acted as a sustaining palliative for previous years of misfortune—but I didn't receive any that I thought unique or jazzy enough to use. I'm not quite sure what I expected. Something like "How Playing Senior Tennis Was Just What I Needed to Smuggle the *Mona Lisa* out of the Louvre"?

More recently, on a visit to Macon, Georgia, in looking for a tennis game I was referred to the John Drew Smith city courts, where an agreeable young woman attendant did indeed set up a game for me. Afterward, before showering, I saw on the club's large bulletin board a notice, calling for a meeting of the "Over 50 Club." Undiscouraged by the blank I had drawn at Princeton to elicit some inspired wisdom from venerable sages of the tennis courts, I thought I'd try again here. So I asked the attendant whom I might contact to get in touch with the Over 50 Club members, in the hope that I might get some material for a book I was writing. She looked somewhat puzzled. "The members of the Over 50 Club? I don't think you could get much for a book from them. Most of them are six or seven years old. You can't be in it if you're over eight."

It was my turn to be taken aback. "Well, what does 'Over 50' mean, then?"

"It's when a small child, taking beginners' tennis lessons, gets to be able to bounce a ball onto the court with his racquet fifty times in a row without missing. Then he or she gets to belong to the Over 50 Club."

I decided to get along without seeking further interviews.

Scanning the sort of programs offered by organizations that specialize in senior play shows that an infinite variety of lower competitive affairs works better than highly competitive, single-elimination tournaments. That sort of tournament is all well and good for deciding real championships, all the way from

133

Wimbledon and Roland Garros and Flushing Meadow to local clubs and community affairs, and there's a place for such tournaments even among seniors, but probably only for those in the super-senior class. They are truly superior older players, most of whom won some tennis recognition as younger competitors, and who now compete fiercely and regularly, traveling from tournament to tournament, aiming for national ratings in their respective age categories. They will scan the announcements each year for such fixtures as the USTA/Volvo League Tennis, the Equitable Family Tennis Challenge, the National Senior Olympics, and the USTA Senior Tennis Council, to determine if they qualify to enter such events. One has to be mighty good to qualify for the last named, for the Senior Tennis Council coordinates and sponsors the teams of seniors that represent the United States in international team play. There's the Bueno Cup for women 50 and up, the Austria Cup for men 55 and up, the Britannia Cup for men 65 and up, and the Crawford Cup for men 70 and up. If you're good enough, and ambitious to try to make a name for yourself in senior tennis, write for the USTA National Senior Sectional Championships tournament schedule, to see what's going on, and where and when. That schedule can be obtained from the USTA office at 1212 Avenue of the Americas, New York, NY 10036.

The rest of us senior tennis players—ordinary mortals of equal enthusiasm but lesser talent—can only wish the best of Methuselah's luck to them. Most of us will fare better, and enjoy ourselves more, in competitions that don't so sharply separate the sheep from the goats. Single-elimination tournaments discourage the players with less than a 3.0 NTRP rating, and tend to bore the one or two who can play at or better than the 5.0 level and who know that inevitably they'll be going to the finals, while everyone else goes home, or at best becomes a spectator.

In such tournaments, at least some element of continuing interest for defeated entries can be obtained by having consolation events in addition to the main draw. This means setting up a new draw for a separate tournament within the main tournament, composed of first-round losers. In a tournament with a very big number of entries, this idea can actually be carried even further, with a separate draw being made up of second-round losers, but that's very rare, and usually one consolation tournament for first-round losers is about all that is justified. Such a practice in a single-elimination tournament assures every entry a minimum of two matches, and an extra chance of some share of glory for those who are beaten at the outset. Sometimes the prizes for the winners of the consolation flight seem just as desirable as those awarded the champions of the main draw.

Single-elimination tournaments are held both for singles and doubles, of course, but the events for seniors that offer the maximum in sociability, enjoyment, and close competition, even if you are not one of the best players, exist in doubles. In case you may not be near a facility that stages such events, or may not be familiar enough with some or all of them to arrange to have them staged in your locality, here's a description of a few of them along with information about them.

ROUND ROBINS

This is by far the most popular, and probably the best way of running a social-mixture tournament. Depending on the size of the field and the number of available courts, it can take a number of forms, but the general idea is something like the "Change partners!" call at a square dance. A doubles partnership plays together as a team for a brief time, usually four games, and then separates, each player hooking up with a new partner against other opponents for the next round, and so on. One form of a well-organized round robin sees to it that, if your partner is a wizard of a player in one round, he'll be one of your opponents in another; similarly, if you've drawn a dodo as partner in one round, he'll be an opponent in another round, and so on. Among the publications put out by the USTA are two that give detailed instructions for running certain types of round robin: *Tennis: Easy-On–Easy-Off* by Eleanor Boland Owens, Item 3011, $3.95, and USTA Senior Recreational Doubles Kit, Item 0700, $5.00. And the *USTA Compass Draw Information Sheet* gives detailed instructions about a round robin type of affair, as well as materials to run the event. That's Item 0504, $.25.

All of these can be obtained from the USTA Publications Department, who put out the *USTA Senior Tennis Directory* and whose address appears on page 128. If you are interested in any of their extensive list of publications and audiovisual materials, write and request their free catalogue. That will not only describe everything that you may want to order, but will inform you of current prices at the time you order.

Meanwhile, to give you an example of how a round robin can work, there follows a portion of an article I once wrote about the subject, which appeared in the May 1975 issue of *World Tennis* and is reprinted here with the kindly concurrence of that magazine. Please note the year—1975—because it explains a couple of things that may trouble you. My son Roger, now a thriving lawyer, was in his last year of high school then. If you ask why neither of us used a personal computer to help work out our problem, the answer is that people didn't have personal computers then. I still don't, and I'm sort of dubious about whether one would have helped, but perhaps it would have. In any event, even with computers abounding these days, I'm not aware that anybody has written such specific instructions about scheduling a round robin since Roger and I had so much fun doing it in our heads. When I wrote the article, I didn't have senior tennis foremost in mind (as is apparent in the second sentence), but I do think the round robin is the ideal format for an enjoyable senior event, so I'm resurrecting the piece for this book:

> The event is called a round robin doubles tournament, and it can be run off from start to

finish in one afternoon's play. Everyone can play in it, from juniors and hoary veterans, through the run-of-the-mill to the best club players. Both sexes. Skill counts heavily, of course, but the luck of the draw counts almost as much, which is why I, in my sixties, have won two trophies recently at such events when I knew there were stronger players in the field. I would not deny that these personal triumphs probably have influenced me to lobby for this type of tournament, but I've honestly enjoyed them almost as much when I finished nowhere in them. Almost as much.

All sorts of variations can be adopted in planning a round robin doubles, but here is a sample scheme for a tournament with 28 entries, which can be run off in something like a couple of hours if you have as many as seven courts. You should have an entry list that is a multiple of four, since there are four players in a doubles match, and you want everyone to be competing in each round of play. If you have only three or four courts, the tournament will take the better part of an afternoon. Even a much bigger entry list—let's say 56—would only double these times and could be fitted into one full day's play.

All right. Your club has decided to conduct such a tournament, and now it's up to the tournament director to figure out how to do it. I can warn you that, unless he (or she) majored in mathematics at MIT, it's virtually certain that the playing schedule devised will not conform

to the ideal pattern for such a tournament—
that no one ever has the same partner, and that
no one ever faces the same opponent in more
than one round.

I played in one of these affairs recently and,
in my innocence, wondered why the planners
of the tournament hadn't been able to figure
out a draw sheet that would satisfy these conditions. It seemed then to be rather an easy
problem to solve, and when I got home that
night I sat down to try it.

Starting logically with horizontal and ver-
tical columns, both listing the numbers as-
signed to each of 28 players, you would think
you could work it out without much sweat, but
this isn't true. Somewhere along the line you
start encountering trouble in the form of repeat
pairings or opponents. At that point you have
to resort to juggling the figures, and attempt
to work it all out by trial and error. I spent
more than an hour and, in the end, had drawn
up a schedule which satisfied the condition that
no one was ever paired with the same partner
or faced the same opponent. But I did sometimes have a person paired with a partner who
had been, or was going to be, an opponent in
another round. This seemed satisfactory to me,
but not to my younger son, Roger, who gets
straight A's in high school math, and who was
peering over my shoulder.

"Why can't you fix it, Dad, so that no one
ever encounters another player in *any* way, except once?"

"Because I'm tired of it all and want to go to bed."

Next morning I found the draw sheet you'll see at the end of this article, which Roger left for me as he went off to school. Beside it was a note that said he had sat up until three in the morning working it out. It had taken that long because he also had to resort to the trial and error technique after a point, but he added that it had been a lot more fun than solving a crossword puzzle.

So Roger and I now dedicate this particular program for running off a tournament of 28 players to any and all in the tennis world who'd like to try it. Obviously, a different draw sheet could be devised, but if you have an entry list of 28, this one will work. If you have a smaller or larger field than that, *you* work it out. With this head start, it shouldn't take you until three in the morning.

With that background, here are the details of how the tournament is conducted. The tournament director makes up 28 separate sheets of paper, numbered from 1 to 28. They are put in a hat and each player draws one out by chance. He retains that number throughout the course of play. He will see that in Round 1 he is partnered with a player with another number, against Number So-and-So and Number Such-and-Such. The same continues to be true in the subsequent rounds, all of which are spelled out on his paper, along with which court each round is to be played upon.

A round consists of four games, which once again makes the concept fair in that each player will be able to serve one game, and one only. In the sample draw given below, five rounds are scheduled. This means that each contestant will play twenty games over the course of the tournament. As he or she completes a round, the number of games *won* in that round is entered on his or her piece of paper: 0, 1, 2, 3, or 4. At the very end of play, these figures are totaled to see which four players have achieved the highest score out of the maximum of 20. It will usually take a total of something between 15 and 20 to be one of these four, and if two or more people are tied in their point totals for earning the fourth spot, they can determine the one to go on to the final by any means decided. That may vary from simply drawing straws to having a brief singles match, like a sudden death play-off.

Now you have four players ready for the final. Once again the pairings are determined by chance: simply let the players draw or spin racquets to determine which two will face the other two. Those two pairs then match off in a final, full set of doubles, to determine which team will be the champions. They might simply play a conventional set with a Tie-Break in case it goes to 6-all, or perhaps an extended professional set to be won by the team first achieving nine games, with a Sudden Death or Tie-Break finish if the score reaches 8-all. This sort of decision is arbitrary and merely depends upon how much play, past the basic 20 games, the tournament director feels the players can take.

That is the way a round robin doubles is held. You will find that the very best players in the field are not at all certain to make the final four contestants. The luck of the draw may doom them to poor partners in the majority or all of the rounds, facing rather good opponents. The worst players in the field probably won't fare too well under any circumstances, but the intermediate ones may easily be fortunate in the draw, consistently having good partners against inferior opponents. So there is absolutely no way to predict the winners beforehand, which is exactly what makes this type of tournament so much more fun for all than a conventional one.

Finally, here is Roger's sample 28-players, five-round schedule:

Round 1:   1 and 2   vs. 15 and 16
              3 and 4   vs. 17 and 18
              5 and 6   vs. 19 and 20
              7 and 8   vs. 21 and 22
              9 and 10 vs. 23 and 24
              11 and 12 vs. 25 and 26
              13 and 14 vs. 27 and 28

Round 2:   1 and 14 vs. 18 and 25
              2 and 17 vs. 19 and 21
              3 and 12 vs. 20 and 23
              4 and 7   vs. 26 and 24
              5 and 8   vs. 16 and 27
              6 and 9   vs. 15 and 28
              10 and 11 vs. 13 and 22

Round 3:   1 and 12 vs. 24 and 27
3 and 9   vs. 22 and 16
25 and 2 vs. 20 and 4
5 and 14 vs. 17 and 26
6 and 11 vs. 21 and 23
7 and 13 vs. 18 and 15
8 and 10 vs. 19 and 28

Round 4: 20 and 28 vs. 11 and 17
2 and 26 vs. 18 and 8
3 and 27 vs. 10 and 15
4 and 12 vs. 13 and 16
5 and 25 vs. 9 and 21
6 and 24 vs. 14 and 22
7 and 23 vs. 19 and 1

Round 5: 2 and 3   vs. 5 and 11
1 and 4   vs. 6 and 10
7 and 9   vs. 12 and 14
8 and 13 vs. 17 and 23
15 and 19 vs. 22 and 25
27 and 26 vs. 20 and 21
24 and 28 vs. 18 and 16

There is surely a mathematical formula which will take care of a field of any size and any number of rounds. If there is, it is beyond our knowledge. If you have a direct line to the ghost of Albert Einstein, I'd suggest you use it.

LADDERS

Ladders are used either for singles or for doubles standings, of course, but we are emphasizing doubles here, and this is a way whereby regular doubles partners can compete against other doubles teams, and establish their place in the doubles rankings of a club, without being constricted by the time demands that invariably complicate a conventional doubles tournament schedule. A board is set up which displays a list of all the teams entered, each pair of names entered on separate cards, in descending order of their ranking. The cards are usually no more than about half an inch high and a couple of inches wide—just big enough to permit two names being posted on them, so the end result looks somewhat like the list of tenants you find in the lobby of an apartment house.

Of course, at the outset the order is set up arbitrarily on the basis of the players' previous reputations, but any injustices can soon be rectified. For each team has the privilege of challenging the team just above it and, in case of a victory, replacing that team on the ladder, with the losers dropping down to the winners' former position. Some ladders permit a team to challenge another two places above; this has much to be said for it since it enables an underrated team to move up more quickly than a crawl, and it offers two possibilities for a challenge rather than only one, which can be most helpful if the team on the ladder just above you never seems to be around on weekends to accept your challenge. Whoever is in charge of the ladder competition, an individual or a committee, makes its own rules about what happens if a challenge is ignored, or delayed beyond reason. Usually, if a challenge is not accepted and a match played within, let's say, two weeks, the challenger wins the match by default, and the teams' positions on the board are exchanged. Nor can a team that has been beaten challenge right back: it has to give the team that has beaten them a chance to move farther on up by playing another match. Of course, if that team is then beaten in its attempt to climb the ladder another notch, it is fair game to be challenged for a return match by the team it beat.

The ladder can be a fairly elaborate board, with metal slots into which cards containing the players' names can be slid and subsequently interchanged as circumstances dictate. That's ideal, but a simple board with protruding nailheads running down vertically, so that tags with holes punched out at the top can be hung from them, will do. The materials with which any ladder is constructed should be fairly sturdy, because ladder competitions go on for quite a long time—often for the entire season—and between handling and weather, if the board is outdoors, flimsy boards and cards won't stand up. As indicated earlier, the great advantage of having a ladder, regardless of what other tournaments may be arranged, is that it's permanent over a considerable period of time, and the rules can be so flexible that players who may have difficulty arranging their affairs to fit into a scheduled

145

tournament can at least remain competitive, against other members of their group, by participating in the ladder.

CENTURY CUP

A final fun doubles event, which involves scurrying around to fix up pairings prior to the event but is worth the trouble, is a century cup tournament. The USTA has a kit for this too, Item 0900, $5.00. It includes everything you need to run an effective event, from a promotional poster to winners' certificates. (I would have thought it might also have told you how to secure duplicate copies of birth certificates, if potential entrants have lost theirs!) For the century cup is simply a traditional elimination doubles tournament, with the intriguing added fillip that the combined ages of the members of each team must equal, or exceed, 100 years!

Certainly it's both an inviting and amusing idea, but what sort of age pairings do you think have the best chance in such a tournament? Initially you might think that a couple of good 50-year-olds would work out best, but mightn't a considerably more active and gifted 35-year-old, partnered with a 65-year-old who is steady as the Rock of Gibraltar, be an even better bet?

Just for fun, suppose we were to conceive a dream

tournament of established stars of the present and the past, all of whom continue to play quality tennis today. Here is one possible entry list of sixteen men, making up eight doubles teams, showing their respective ages and the teams' totals. Record books vary a bit in giving birth dates, and it's possible there's an error of a year one way or the other in a player's age, but no more than that, I'm pretty sure, and in any case the principle remains the same, even if there's a team in the draw whose combined ages add up only to 99 years. Who's going to demand that the case be taken to the Supreme Court?

Boris Becker (23) and Gardnar Mulloy (77)	100 years
Mats Wilander (26) and Frankie Parker (74)	100 years
Ivan Lendl (30) and Bobby Riggs (72)	102 years
John McEnroe (31) and Tom Brown (69)	100 years
Björn Borg (34) and Vic Seixas (67)	101 years
Jimmy Connors (37) and Frank Sedgman (63)	100 years
Cliff Drysdale (48) and Ken Rosewall (56)	104 years
Rod Laver (52) and Fred Stolle (52)	104 years

Which team do you think would win? Which would be the runner-up? Which the other two semifinalists?

Is there any one team that you think wouldn't have a chance? I don't think so. I don't know who would win, but what a fabulously interesting event it would be!

Sadly, such a tournament almost surely will never take place, the economics of major tennis stars being what it is. There wouldn't be enough money involved. But century cup tournaments are quite practical for local tennis, and offer new vistas for the ambitious over-50 player or over 60 . . . or 70 . . . or ? . . . I've figured it out. Some years from now, when my oldest grandchild, Alex, will be 15, I'll be 85! I can hardly wait!

ACKNOWLEDGMENTS

Eugene L. Scott is the person who put the idea of writing this book into my head when, in one of his editorials in *Tennis Week*, he wrote, "Have you ever seen a bona fide book for seniors offering to make the game more fun for older players? I'd settle for an article." Well, Gene, I've tried to make this such a book and I hope you like it.

Also, although this is a very personal and even an opinionated book, I've spent so many years playing tennis, discussing tennis, and reading about tennis that some observations and ideas of others have seeped into my consciousness as having particular merit and, getting permission wherever necessary or simply courteous, I pass them along to the reader of this book. In particular I am grateful to Simon & Schuster for permission to excerpt and adapt material from *Total Fitness in 30 Minutes a Week*, by Laurence E. Morehouse and Leonard Gross, and to Henry Holt and Company for an excerpt from *Gamesmanship*, by Stephen Potter. The United States Tennis Association was most cooperative in allowing me to quote from its *Senior Tennis Directory*, and *World Tennis* extended its blessing for my reprinting a piece of my own that I once wrote for that magazine. In the case of more casual bits of wisdom that have impressed me, notably those of Dick Bradlee, Jack Barnaby, and Gene Scott, acknowledgment is made in the text where they appear.

If subliminally I've encroached on somebody else's brainchild, I regret not realizing it, and in my defense can only quote Rudyard Kipling once again:

> When 'Omer smote his bloomin' lyre,
> He'd 'eard men sing by land an' sea;
> An' what 'e thought 'e might require,
> 'E went an' took—the same as me!